expansive treatment from the diarist, but his first aim should always be to condense and record without the loss of intensity or detail.

Part of my interest in diary-writing as a style was the fact that events which on the surface are very different in scale or importance can be given equal place in the day's entry. This was certainly true of Woodforde; he might record the burial of a child – a sad morning's duty – and then go on to describe, with equal simplicity and character, a boisterous luncheon. This was not tactless or inappropriate juxtaposition, but a quite valid technique, which was particularly useful to me since I was trying to tie together a great number of events related to the experience of food, sometimes quite directly but often not. I doubt if I could have done this without the diarist's discipline and special skills.

Of course a book has to have its limits, and I have deliberately excluded certain areas of experience; politics and world events are absent and there is less detail about the characters themselves than some people might expect. But I have included a good deal about the countryside, firstly to record events and impressions that will give some idea of the flow of the seasons, and secondly to put the diary into its true landscape, to provide a background to the events that form the main part of the book. This is also the aim of the Introduction; it sets the scene, it is a kind of 'verbal map' describing my locality, its character and its people.

Soon after I began the diary it occurred to me that, rather than reflecting my eating habits, it might in fact begin to dictate them. I might begin to contrive meals simply to give myself something to write about. But this has not been the case. It is a simple record of how I have used food, and how it has affected me over two years. My main hope now is that it reads brightly; that it is authentic, evocative and amusing.

At the time when I began to write the book, Rose and I were in a situation that was both ordinary and uncommon. Like many young married couples we could not afford to buy a house, so we were living as caretakers in a cottage belonging to my brother Richard. We had little money and living where we did our sources of supply were limited – we relied a great deal on garden produce, hedgerow food and meaty gifts from friends and relatives. I was working part-time as a gardener while I carried on with my writing; this arrangement had disadvantages – mainly financial insecurity – but it also provided me with the time and facilities to observe, experiment and study food. And from the very beginning we had to live within limits, we had to work out a system of economy based on resourcefulness, ingenuity and good planning. Had I been working at a regular job, the themes and content of the book would have been very different. As it was, the balance between gardening, cooking and eating was immensely important to the continuity I was trying to achieve.

Introduction

The village of Wenhaston is split by a road. To the south there are clusters of old cottages and a few important large houses; to the north, new bungalows and a small housing estate. The road begins, at its western end, with an old and rather too picturesque pub that was originally a smuggling headquarters. As you cross the road you will pass over the remains of a tunnel that once linked the pub with the near-by church; this was the escape route when smugglers needed to hide and dispose of their goods quickly.

The road into the village starts flat and straight; it passes the relics of the railway station – originally a stopping-point for the local trains from Southwold to Halesworth – and on either side are meadows with willows and alders which back onto the river. This is the Blyth, although by the time it reaches Wenhaston it is little more than a stream. The road lifts over the river and then turns sharply uphill. Here are the first houses, and as the road levels out, on the right, is our cottage.

It is a sturdy, imposing brick and flint place built about 200 years ago, and used for the most part as the local rectory. There is a useful garden, full of fruit bushes, fruit trees – apples, pears, a cherry that is sterile and an ancient greengage – also healthy asparagus and strawberry beds. The garden explodes with a huge collection of bulbs in the spring, herbs creep over the rose-beds and concrete paths, and birds feed well off our produce. Around the cottage are scattered pieces of farmland; a wheat field backs steeply onto our garden, and this field is yearly decimated by rabbits and birds. In the spring, when it is green with young wheat, huge bare patches appear overnight as the rabbits begin to devour the shoots. The field is also the haunt of field-mice which invade our house, and join with house-mice to create havoc; they fight in the attic, eat their way through knotholes in the floorboards, shred magazines and forage in the kitchen.

Near by there are sugar-beet fields, meadows, grassy walks and lanes lined with hedgerow fruit – sloes, haws, blackberries, hips. But the real character of this area is in the heath. It is rough country, often blazing yellow with broom and gorse flowers, and in summer it is hot, dry and dusty; adders lurk here. If the village has a centre it is the heath. Age, wildness and paths hacked through tall bracken are its true features. On a June night you may hear a nightingale calling from the awkward branches of a crab-apple tree, or see a still nightjar, the extension of a dead branch, suddenly burst into flight, taking flies on the wing. But by December much of the area is blackened and dead, for each year it is the village custom to fire the heath on Guy Fawkes Night. The place is called Blackheath.

But there are other, very different landscapes not far away.

Move eastwards through Wenhaston towards the coast and soon you are among marsh meadows and saltings – the estuary of the river Blyth. Clustered along the estuary is the village of Blythburgh, shadowed by its vast, ornate church; across the road from this is the White Hart, my favourite pub.

Alternatively you can go south-east out of Wenhaston and this way pass through dark conifer forests on the way to Dunwich. This was once a thriving port which boasted no fewer than nine churches. But the place was literally built on sand, and since the Middle Ages it has fallen, bit by bit, into the sea. The cliffs still slide, and the village now consists of a pub, a new church and a few cottages. The virtue of the place is that you can go down to the beach and buy freshly caught sprats, cod and soles straight from the boats. And you can crunch your way along the shingle, picking up driftwood for the fire, and watch the guillemots.

Between the marshy Blyth estuary and the Dunwich forests, there is more heathland – the marvellous Newdelight Walks – and thick patches of reeds. Here I have seen silent marsh harriers and heard distant booming bitterns.

There is one more important road out of Wenhaston. It turns south-west, inland towards the next village, Bramfield. We take this road when we go shopping, for Bramfield has an excellent butcher and an amazingly well-stocked village supermarket. We go over the high ground through sheep pasture and sugar-beet fields; this is the short road and we are soon in the village. After the shopping is done we can take the other road home; this snakes around the sloping fields, past the dairy, and up a lane that is always dark. Then back into Wenhaston. But by now it is getting late, and there is a meal to be cooked.

Monday 25 December 1972. Christmas. A grey, still morning; normally such dreary weather would keep us in bed, brooding, but today we woke and got up full of energy and enthusiasm. We ignored the weather.

My presents from Rose included a jar of Indian bamboo pickle, which came to my rescue soon after breakfast; I was feeling rather queasy, so I took a medicinal spoonful of this to revive me. I always find the effect of chillies most valuable although it gives rise to much eye-watering. The pickle was sharp and deceptively mild, but with an unexpected, agonizing aftertaste.

We were to spend the holiday with Rose's parents, so we set out for Blakeney on the north Norfolk coast, our ancient car filled up with presents and food, and we arrived in plenty of time for lunch. A large turkey (about 20 lb), roasted with pieces of bacon and an aromatic stuffing of herbs, onions and chopped bacon, all eaten with roast potatoes, peas, mashed swedes and sprouts. There is something very reassuring about the predictable pleasures of Christmas dinner, and this vast meal was equal to all my expectations. But the occasion shouldn't simply be an excuse for indiscriminate gorging and gluttony, rather an opportunity to make use of special kitchen skills that have been stockpiled throughout the year. This kind of tradition needs to be maintained and even extended for other occasions. We must find foods to suit the day.

After lunch the weather cleared and we ambled out onto the marshes. It was a shining winter's afternoon with a violent icy wind blowing in from the sea; we instinctively curled our bodies and put up coat collars to protect ourselves. Blakeney seemed to be alive with activity – families out walking, dogs splashing in the freezing water and overhead the sound of screaming gulls. This was familiar country. As we walked back towards the quayside, our path was flanked on the left by the marshes, cut by a maze of reedy pools and channels, an area that always retains the luxuriant green of a summer meadow. On our right the view was very different: the winding waterway from the quay out to Blakeney Point. This was grey, muddy and barren, and only coloured by the sail of an occasional small boat or the fluorescent yellow of an oilskin.

We reached the quay with its odd assortment of boats, most of which are the temporary homes of summer visitors, and then climbed the steep hill – literally the high street – past the pub and on towards Sidney the butcher. Opposite his shop stands the little cottage where my brother and I and a crowd of friends spent weeks and weekends drinking, bird-watching and cooking. Strangers live in the cottage now, and the gang has broken up, but the place still has power enough to evoke those days.

Finally we arrived back at Rose's parents' cottage, exhausted and still weighed down with lunch; the walk had done little to relieve us. Later, about nine in the evening, someone suggested supper and we reluctantly agreed. It is the custom that Rose's father prepares this meal, and he vanished into the kitchen to perform his duties. It wasn't long before he reappeared with plates of cold turkey, pickles and a salad of raw cabbages; these were strange, being no bigger than large sprouts, but fully formed. We drank liberal quantities of home-brewed beer, sampling the virtues of bitter, lager and barley wine. By the end of the evening we were all very merry; it had been a pleasant day, a true celebration.

Wednesday 27 December. We had intended to go back to Suffolk today, but our plans were altered, almost inevitably, by the needs of Rose's ponies. A makeshift stable was needed on the mare's field, so I volunteered to help Rose's brother put up the structure.

This was exhausting work, but we were revived by a welcome Broadside at noon. The Broadside is a recent invention, a commemorative beer brewed by Adnams – the local Suffolk brewery – to mark the tercentenary of the Battle of Sole Bay. This was a bloody, indecisive affair between the British and the Dutch navy which ended as a pointless draw. The beer that they brewed to celebrate this occasion must rate as one of the strongest ever produced in a bottle. It is certainly potent, but I have never found it at all unpleasant, and today it spurred me on to greater feats of strength and endurance; a real restorative.

By the end of the afternoon we had finished the job, and I returned home to rest myself in a hot bath with a glass of malt whisky. Feeling much refreshed I ate a very large supper: a beautiful piece of brisket roasted with onions and eaten with swedes baked in the juices from the meat. Finished with a glass of velvet twenty-year-old port and a fat cigar.

Friday 29 December. Back to Wenhaston to get ready for our New Year visitors: my brother Richard, Fran, Alastair, 'Mouse' and Alan with baby Thomas. Rose made a bacon and mushroom pie with a cheap hock, followed by a sturdy jam sponge. We had to let the bulk of this meal subside before going up to the Blythburgh White Hart to sample the mild.

Put the bone of the hock to simmer with some split peas; soup for tomorrow.

Saturday 30 December. A bright, clear morning. The sunlight, pouring in through our dining-room window, dazzled us as we ate our breakfast. Afterwards we decided to take a walk, but Alan and I, not the most dedicated bird-watchers, returned before lunch after hearing whooper swans booming across the marshes. Home to the split-pea soup, which was yellow and thick like blancmange. The others missed this but came back with tales of hen harriers and sparrowhawks.

We talked of holding a beer and pickle party, invited friends and travelled to Southwold for supplies. While we were out, Rose produced an enormous oblong pizza.

Our solid dining table loaded up with cold meats, the pizza, salads, bread, several cheeses and a chocolate sponge with pears

David Mabey

Breadlines

A journal of food and events

Illustrations by David Goddard

Allen Lane

First published in 1975

ALLEN LANE
Penguin Books Ltd
17 Grosvenor Gardens
London SW1

ISBN 0 7139 0763 0

Typeset in Plantin by Typesetting Services Ltd, Glasgow
Printed in Great Britain by
Butler & Tanner Ltd., Frome and London

for Hannah

Preface

I began work on this journal at the end of 1972. In fact the idea originated with Rose, who thought it might be interesting to record the food that we ate throughout the year; she had in mind a kind of personal recipe book, but I was much more taken with the notion of a diary in which I could explore all the different factors that affect our food and eating habits.

Food – and for me that includes drink as well – is a complicated subject. It doesn't begin or end with the meal on the dinner table, but it is an intricate fabric of moods, influences and responses. It is affected by the weather, by supplies in the larder, by the inevitable movement of the seasons. And food is not all success and interest either; there are disasters, times when you have to improvise, when you simply don't feel like cooking or can't decide what to give friends who are coming to visit you. At the furthest extreme we have to admit that food is sometimes little more than a boring necessity. What I have tried to do is to record all these different aspects of food and to present a complete and convincing picture of my eating habits.

I chose to write the book in the form of a diary for several reasons. To begin with I was greatly influenced by some of the diarists of the past, notably Parson Woodforde and Gilbert White. Woodforde was undoubtedly my main model, but White's reflective writing, his concise style and acute sense of detail also affected me. I felt it was important that the book should have direction and continuity, and the chronological form of the diary helped to reinforce this. While each entry is quite detailed and there is a great deal of variety, I hope that a larger pattern emerges: that of a 'year's turning', month following month and season following season. To highlight this aspect of the book I decided to include two yearly cycles to expose both the similarities and the differences between them.

The actual process of writing the diary was an odd mixture of informal jottings and, later, a disciplined reworking of the original notes. Sometimes I would write an entry at the end of the day, while on other occasions I needed to distance myself from events before I could begin to write about them; it was often much easier to capture the true atmosphere or mood of an occasion after I had thought about it for a few days. Occasionally I needed to fill out the material, but usually it was a matter of paring down in an attempt to reach the essentials of the day. The greatest talent of the old diary-writers, apart from their powers of observation, was their ability to condense all the feelings, moods and events of a day into a single phrase, sentence or paragraph; they had a special and remarkable talent for manipulating language. Sometimes the scale of events demands a larger, more which was buried in chocolate sauce and whirls of whipped cream. I laid out an impressive selection of pickles and chutneys including a special jar of 'marrow mangoes'; Alastair, eating pieces of marrow and pickled eggs whole, sweated badly.

A subdued, erratic evening. Most of us feeling the effects of coughs and colds and the looming 'flu bug. Consumed a fair quantity of drink but hardly merry; Richard was uneasy throughout the party, and his efforts at forced jollity meant that the carpet had to cope with a great spillage of food and Broadsides.

Sunday 31 December. Another marvellous, spring-like morning; felt surprisingly well after last night's activities. On a morning such as this there is only one possible breakfast – kippers. These came from Southwold and were smoked by the fishmonger himself: 'Those big firms, they don't *smoke* them!' he once said. This simple epitaph on much of our so-called 'smoked' fish was all the more convincing because it came from a man who knew his trade.

After breakfast I set about opening the jar of Moutarde de Meaux that I had given Richard as a belated Christmas present. This comes in a squat stoneware jar, sealed with a cork and red wax. I managed to chip away the wax and prise out the cork with my fish-knife; inside there was roughly ground mustard seed, still husked, and held in wine vinegar.

Later out for a long walk; a pair of marsh harriers seen patrolling the reeds over Walberswick marshes. Back to one of Rose's expert vegetable soups and the relics of yesterday's party food. Richard and Fran were occupied in the kitchen for most of the afternoon. I was looking forward to this meal – a crown of lamb roasted with oranges – but it turned out to be the least successful food of the holiday. The lamb was badly underdone and served with a pan of assorted vegetables cooked in their own juice – an insipid and uninteresting mixture. This was a real disappointment since Richard *can* cook with skill and imagination. In all a meal best forgotten.

To the White Hart for New Year's Eve after much arguing. Pints of mild and free food – hot roast potatoes, bits of smoked salmon on crispy fried bread, pastry horns filled with scrambled egg, mince pies. Before midnight the sound of bagpipes far away: a solitary piper in the pub car-park, calling in the New Year.

Monday 1 January 1973. Alastair looked terrible and we ordered him to bed; he was shivering with the 'flu. But as he slept during the morning, Alan played a mischievous trick on him. He put the radio outside Alastair's bedroom door as it played Chopin's funeral march, and when Alastair woke, roused by the pulse of the music, he almost believed his time had come.

Tuesday 2 January. Richard was planning a pheasant supper for the end of the holiday, when most of our friends had gone home and he could reasonably afford it. He had seen tempting Jerusalem artichokes and salad vegetables in Southwold and had contrived a splendid feast.

But it was a gloomy day, full of mishaps. The weather was foggy, and everyone went home, leaving Alastair still bedridden; Richard said we would need the pheasant if only to cheer ourselves up and pass away the dismal hours. He was ready to go to

Southwold, and then found his car wouldn't start. So eventually he went with Rose to Halesworth, abandoning thoughts of a well-planned meal. Everything now depended on what he could get in Halesworth, but, as it turned out, he found some pheasant and also bought some fat leeks and an expensive out-of-season cucumber (20p).

The cooking went well. The whole meal consisted of roast pheasant and leeks, with some cucumber and tomato salad. As we had no vinegar in the house, I suggested an improvised dressing using some of the horseradish vinegar which was steeping in the pickle cupboard. And as a final touch I put out some basil jelly (or rather apple jelly flavoured with basil) instead of the more usual redcurrant.

Wednesday 3 January. Stricken with the 'flu, but enjoyed a bowl of pheasant soup made from the bones of yesterday's meal.

Richard and Alastair left for home, ashen-faced and trembling.

Saturday 6 January. Travelled down to Berkhamsted to spend the weekend with my mother and Richard, who had almost recovered from a plethora of real and contrived illnesses.

In my old haunt, the Swan, drank some bitter, the first for several months. After the silky potency of the Suffolk mild, this was metallic, gassy and almost undrinkable; it also costs an extra 4p a pint. On reflection it may have been a blessing that my taste-buds were still numbed by the remnants of a cold.

Monday 8 January. Back to Suffolk on the slow coach.

Friday 12 January. Food prices are soaring, and I think there is trouble ahead, but I consoled myself that our four young chickens would at least supply us with all the eggs we needed once their combs had reddened.

However, this morning I glanced out towards the chicken run and sensed that all was not well; it was no more than a feeling of unease, but when I went to feed them my worst suspicions were confirmed. On the lawn was a grey trail of feathers. Three of the chickens lay under the pear tree, reduced to lifeless bundles; another was still inside the run. There had been a bloodless struggle, and I suspect that the chickens were playfully killed by an overfed domestic labrador; its tracks were everywhere. If this had been the work of a predatory fox or stoat, I could have accepted the slaughter more easily, but the stupid violence of a domestic animal only angers me.

Afternoon: shopping in Southwold. Damp, depressing weather. Made a blunder in the butcher's shop; I was looking for some hand of pork for our Sunday lunch, they had none, and I carelessly accepted a piece of loin, little more than a pound and costing 50p. (I think I was distracted by the sight of the butcher drawing a chicken with half a dozen swift, confident movements.) But it was too late, I had paid the price, and when I confessed my mistake to Rose, she swore that the pork would have to last us three days.

I can recall only one image from this morning's events: our cultivated fennel graced with a new plumage – feathers trapped like flies in the green web of its leaves.

Sunday 14 January. The first of the pork eaten fried with creamed potatoes, fried parsnips and apple sauce. I suggested a cup of strong ground coffee to finish off the meal – a welcome change from our daily 'instant'.

Monday 15 January. Roasted the rest of the pork and used part of it in a near duplication of yesterday's meal. Imagination a little lacking today.

Rose has plans for the remainder.

Tuesday 16 January. Rose was right, the pork will last. Her will-power sustains our economy, and her imagination transforms our often meagre supplies; we have learned to eat cheaply. Tonight she produced a substantial concoction – a white sauce holding chopped pork, mushrooms, gherkins, all encased in a weighty pancake.

Sunday 21 January. Rose's parents visiting us today, no idea what to cook for them. Meat and poultry prices have soared, so conventional roasts are out of the question. Eventually decided on a liver casserole made from a pound of pig's liver (28p) and a 4p hock of bacon. It was one of those meals where the sheer quantity and bulk of the food was as important as its taste. Casseroles ought to be made to fill a large pot, otherwise they simply do not work. We enjoyed the meal because we could demand several helpings and watch the mixture being heaped onto our plates with a ladle.

As the weather forecasters predicted, it looks as if we are in for a spell of fine weather. A brilliant clear day, sun warm but a strong cutting wind; it could be March. Rose's father tells me he has seen elder bushes in Blakeney with full green shoots.

Rose's parents are generous in an honest, simple way. Because Mac is in the agricultural business he often gets us sacks of potatoes and carrots, but he also raids his own deep-freeze, and regularly produces joints of rare mutton and boiling fowls – casualties from his own stock of chickens. Today he brought a chicken and also a piece of frozen pork; we will eat the chicken this week, and store the pork in a friend's deep-freeze.

Monday 22 January. The bone from yesterday's hock stood overnight, soaking with some dried peas (no split peas in the house). Made soup. The peas were very ancient and needed a great deal of slow cooking before they softened. I visited the pot during the afternoon and threw in a few bay leaves and coriander seeds, and by tea time the soup was ready for straining. I pulled the bone and pieces of rind out of the saucepan and sucked the juice; it was gelatinous, fatty and sweet, and felt like glue sticking to my lips and chin. The soup very good, a little salty for Rose, but even so tasty and much to my liking.

Saturday 27 January. In the afternoon I painted our kitchen. It now looks renewed, an encouraging place to work in. Rose bought me two large plaice roes for my supper, which I managed to cook, manoeuvring around misplaced bits of furniture. These roes have more texture than taste, so I decided to make a mustard sauce for them while they were frying. The combination of the thick, strong sauce with the roe (crisp and sweet on the outside, the inside white like mouthfuls of tiny soft pearls) was exactly right.

In good spirits as I have organized my gardening work for the year.

Tuesday 30 January. My birthday. Rose travelled to Beccles and returned with presents for me – a book and a lemon sole for my supper. I had to venture into the garden with a candle to search for parsley; the evening was black so I gathered it by feeling and peering into the dark.

We ate seated up at the table for the first time in several weeks. In these dark months we usually gather round the fire with plates on our laps.

Sunday 4 February. We have almost come through the winter, and the new season seems to be advancing very fast. In our garden there are snowdrops, primroses and the first crocuses challenging the frost. Fruit bushes with buds not yet taken by our pair of princely bullfinches. The green shoots of chives showing through the blanket of dead blanched stems; a regular sign of approaching spring.

I must dig and manure our vegetable patch ready for this year's crops.

Friday 9 February. Today the warmest and most glorious day of the year so far; I now wait eagerly for some really hot weather. Started my work as a gardener. One of the great pleasures of hard gardening is the appetite for large meals and numerous pints of beer that it produces. There will be some good summer drinking soon.

Tuesday 13 February. Hopes of an early spring dashed. Woke this morning to find the weather bitterly cold and sleeting. It is a time for broth. Tonight a beautiful chicken stew – the perfect heavy, fatty meal for this bone-chilling weather. Monster potatoes baked in their jackets and wedged with chunks of butter.

Saturday 17 February. Rose's parents here for the day. There is a special job to be done – fencing off a field in Blythburgh where Rose will keep the ponies. Left a joint of bacon simmering in the pot while we went out. After driving in stakes with a sledge-hammer, I was in need of a pint, so we dashed to the near-by White Hart, confident that the lunch would not spoil. As I had predicted, it was perfect when we arrived home. A glorious meal of bacon, split peas, carrots (sugared and buttered) with sweet Desirée potatoes. The rind of the bacon had become quite soft during cooking, in fact I ate most of it myself.

Wednesday 21 February. These gloomy days give me time to think of events later in the year: the planting of seeds, the first asparagus and strawberries, salads. There will be celebrations, visits to the Butley Oysterage, perhaps venison in Scotland, and always good beer and Broadsides. Autumn will find us gathering sloes and blackberries, and I shall be seen digging for horseradish or rescuing fallen crab-apples from the side of the road.

And then, once again, it will be Christmas.

Thursday 1 March. Richard coming up tomorrow. Slight problems deciding what to cook for him as a welcoming meal. Nothing too overpowering because there will doubtless be some heavy drinking in the evening. Rose given an old boiling fowl in return for some baby-sitting; I will use this cooked with herbs and smothered in mushroom sauce.

Friday 2 March. Richard very relieved to be up in Suffolk again after several months' not very fruitful work. He offered to help with the meal and I gave him the task of peeling the mushrooms. Disaster – they were dripping with some ancient putrefaction like pine rosin and the whole lot had to be thrown away. I had to think quickly, but soon decided on a sauce made from pickled plums; this was an impulsive stroke, but the sauce was easy and quick to make. I used the sweetened and spiced vinegar from the pickle with some of the pulped plum flesh, and added orange juice and a little mustard. After blending and heating this mixture, I thickened it so that it was almost solid and could be spread over the rather dry chicken. It was an exotic, oriental combination, and it helped to make the meal a success. Richard, in good form, ate a vast amount and was then eager to go to the pub to sample the beer.

He drank very well, the taste of Adnams after months of keg bitter was too great a temptation and he had consumed several pints before the evening was done, to such an extent that he raided our spice shelves when we returned home, and proceeded to stuff neat sesame seeds and dried chillies without flinching.

Saturday 3 March. Steaks. On the occasion of Rose's birthday Richard gave us huge rare steaks, spread with a fiery *au poivre* sauce. He laid these on our plates, and came round the table with a pan full of ratatouille in which the tomatoes and onions had softened to a purée, leaving aubergines and green peppers intact. And finally jacket potatoes dressed with chervil filched from the garden. Can hardly recall when we last ate steak – it must have been last summer. We celebrated the meal in the Harbour Inn at Southwold, an old quayside pub famed for its dim lighting, bar billiards and a jazz band made up of fishermen, house-painters and itinerant musicians. Had beery aftertastes of the food throughout the evening.

Walking on the quay at closing time, I remembered that I shall become a father later this month; sobering reflections after a drunken night.

Sunday 4 March. A fine plump kipper for breakfast – now an established custom in this house on a bright Sunday morning. I enjoy the prospect of boning the fish, with its satisfying feeling of neat surgery: first remove the head (contrary to the belief that kippers exist only as frozen, bony fillets), peel off the main central bone and the fabric of smaller bones, finally pull off the crisp tail fin. The fish is now exposed, and spread with butter and mustard it's a meal without equal.

Thursday 15 March. Richard returned. He has offered to stay and keep me company while Rose is in hospital having the baby.

Friday 16 March. A long evening's drinking; the flow of ale set me reminiscing about early culinary experiments, including my first *ghobi* prawn – an astonishing dry curry made from prawns and cauliflower. I rather rashly suggested I should like to cook this dish again during the weekend.

Saturday 17 March. This morning – sober again – I appeared to be fully committed to the *ghobi* prawn. Richard and I had planned on sharing the cooking over the weekend, so we visited Southwold to get supplies. I bought a pint of fresh prawns for 30p, and also a large cauliflower. Richard was thinking of a fish speciality too; a vast chunk of fresh cod baked with green grapes. He procured the first new potatoes of the year.

The cod was some of the best I have tasted, it was soft and sweet like whiting. But something very odd happens to grapes when they are cooked; they become like stewed plums or greengages. I should like to use them more often in cooking.

The potatoes were not quite 'new'; they were floury and there was an oldness about them. But Richard's real master-stroke was to serve chicory as part of the meal; its bitter flavour perfectly balanced the sweetness of the fish and grapes. However, he had forgotten about its potency as a diuretic, and we were all getting up through the night to relieve ourselves.

In the pub during the evening I planned my curry for tomorrow and mentioned the possibilities of using red kidney beans, but forgot to put them to soak overnight.

Sunday 18 March. Early morning and Rose declared that the birth was beginning. Lumbered downstairs, half asleep, desperately trying to grasp the reality of the situation after so many months of waiting. Made tea and toasted sandwiches for us both, and remembered to put the beans in to soak although I fully expected that the curry would have to be postponed. Rose at home all day and by 6 in the evening we were faced with two crucial decisions – the hospital and the fate of the curry. We agreed on a deadline of 7 o'clock, so Richard and I set about preparing the swiftest curry ever. I spent the time rushing between the kitchen and sitting-room, testing spices and checking Rose's condition; it had become a race in deadly earnest. Luckily the *ghobi* prawn is an easy curry to make and I hurled spices, coconut and tomatoes into the pan with the confident intuition that dictates all my curries, while Richard dealt with shelling the prawns, quickly thawed in hot water, but not ruined by this technique.

After we had 'thrown' the *ghobi* together, I devised an Indian–Mediterranean crossbreed using the beans with green peppers, tomatoes, mushrooms, paprika and cummin seed. Time getting short, we ate the curries in great haste and left for the hospital just after 7 o'clock with enough food on the table for tomorrow.

At 10 o'clock I was drinking cocoa with Rose in the labour ward while I waited with her. It was to be a long night – I was very tired and there was not much progress.

Monday 19 March. Another day of hard labour. Rose seemed to be making good progress and it looked as if she might give birth in the evening; returned home and reheated yesterday's food for an early supper.

When I cook I invariably dish myself out the largest portion of food – I usually have the largest appetite and a disguised sense of greed, which is recognized as the cook's privilege. But today I gave myself the smaller portion, ensuring that Richard had the best part of the meal. Lack of sleep and the scale of events had wrecked my appetite and I was dogged by visions of passing out in the heat of the labour ward, and imagined myself in a state of unbearable queasiness – a reaction to the powerful physicality of the birth process. As it turned out these fears were unfounded.

Tuesday 20 March. After spending another night at the hospital, I was beginning to feel the effects of lack of sleep; by morning I was vulnerably low and had difficulty in keeping my eyes open. At 9 o'clock the doctor arrived and told me that Rose would have to be moved to the maternity hospital at Norwich. This news hit me hard. I imagined all the worst consequences of a difficult birth, and feared for Rose and the baby. I had managed to maintain confidence and patience during the labour, and had kept a sense of detachment and rationality. In a moment this was gone, and I was simply scared.

The considerate nurses insisted that I ought to eat breakfast before setting off for Norwich, but the sight of a lightly boiled egg and dark syrupy tea only aggravated my condition. However I managed to force down a piece of toast and marmalade. It was one of the few occasions when I have been almost completely unable to face food. Lack of sleep, my nervous state and the tactless symbolism of the egg combined to produce a feeling of sickly revulsion.

But my anxieties vanished as quickly as they had appeared; the sheer excitement of the ambulance ride to Norwich was enough to clear my head and restore my confidence. The sirens wailed, and cars mounted the pavement as we jolted around roadworks and through red traffic lights. Then up in the lift to the tenth floor of the hospital, where Rose was moved to a delivery room, and I was dressed in a surgeon's white coat and mask.

The ride must have affected Rose, for I was soon called in to help with the delivery. My main impression was of very hard work, of supreme physical effort. Rose was straining every muscle while I wiped her brow with a cloth and urged her on to further exertions. We were both hot and excited. The delivery had the mounting exhilaration of travelling very fast in an open car. And then the head was out, the first cry, and it was all over. At eight minutes to twelve we had a daughter. Rose had been in the hospital less than two hours.

Richard had loyally travelled to Norwich and when I emerged from the delivery room he was waiting. I was smiling, with tears in my eyes and sweat pouring from me, so when he produced a half bottle of whisky, I drank hardly noticing the sting of the liquor. We left Rose resting exhausted and had a quick lunch of beer and pickled eggs before returning to Wenhaston. Neither of us had the energy to cook a substantial supper, so Richard bought lambs' kidneys which we grilled and ate on toast with a tomato and onion salad. Drank some cheap red wine – the remains of a bottle that had seen Richard through the long nights of Sunday and Monday.

After drinking a good quantity of wine and some whisky, we went to Gordon's for a small celebration. Drank more whisky and Richard sampled their potent Tunisian fig liqueur. Finished off with Malmsey and the best egg sandwiches I've ever tasted, made with fresh wholemeal bread, still warm. To bed beautifully drunk and happy.

Wednesday 21 March. Visited Rose in Norwich, and took the opportunity of looking round the Mustard Shop that Colman's have recently established in the city. A quiet, elegant place decorated like an old emporium, with velvet curtains and thick maroon carpets. The manager, immaculate in a dark dinner suit and red carnation buttonhole. The entire shop is devoted to mustard, its history and uses; there are big tins of veterinary mustard, Victorian advertisements and samples showing the ingredients of the prepared product from the days when mustard was thickened with ground rice. They do not stock whole mustard seed, but all varieties of ground mustard, packed and sold like coffee in cartons made of thick brown paper.

Thursday 29 March. Rose home from hospital; her mother here to help with the first few days of motherhood. Gales threatening to rip the roof off our garage and uproot our may tree, so I had to go out with ropes and concrete blocks to anchor it.

I have noticed that wild fennel is appearing along all the sandy roadside banks. Although road-widening is now a feature of this area, these plants seem to have survived the bulldozer; they are far too resilient to be obliterated by such schemes.

Saturday 31 March. Saw a magnificent barn owl as I was cycling down the A12. It appeared in the cloudless sky and floated almost motionless above me. I was in the predator's eye, and for an instant sensed that I could be the object of the hunt. Out on the

road, I felt as vulnerable as any field-mouse; it was greatly unnerving.

Friday 6 April. Mac came down to pick up Barbara. We had bought a haggis from the local butcher as a surprise for him; in fact an immigrant Scot who lives in our area makes them. It is encouraging to find that such skills are put to good use, and that the butcher rejects the easy solution of tinned haggis; the can is really no substitute for the sheep's belly.

There are many tricks for cooking a haggis; it must be brought to the boil very slowly, and 'suspended' at a temperature just below boiling-point, otherwise the skin bursts and the contents of the haggis spill out. I thought I had the measure of this technique, but while peeling some potatoes I checked the pot and noticed that the skin had in fact started to split. I had to act swiftly. With Barbara's help I managed to get it out of the saucepan intact, onto a piece of foil, and into a colander; finished cooking it by steaming.

Carried the haggis to the table. The sight of it made Mac smile. We served it with piles of mashed potatoes and tinned processed peas, which are a good substitute for the traditional swedes or turnips. The food should be heavy, with a feeling of bulk, and delicate petit pois or garden peas would be hopelessly inappropriate in these circumstances. We had the remains of a bottle of whisky that had fortified us during the week; there was just enough left for a nip with the haggis. The contrast between the high-powered, intense drink and the thick mouthfuls of food made the lure of this combination quite understandable; it was easy to see why it originated.

A gargantuan meal, but after half an hour's solid, steady eating there was little of it left. We stuffed ourselves in silence and rose from our seats with difficulty.

Sunday 8 April. First vegetable planting today. Rather late but the weather has been so appalling over the past few weeks, with tree-wrecking gales, torrential rain and frosts, that there had been little chance of doing anything in the garden, except essential digging.

The morning fine and clear, so I planted some early Epicure potatoes and maincrop Desirée. Then the weather turned, and I sowed onion sets and broad beans between brief snow showers. But tonight the snow is falling fast and covering the ground.

Friday 13 April. The White Hart has changed hands. I called in for a lunch-time pint and to see the new landlord.

The Hart was originally a medieval courthouse and later a coaching inn. It stands beside a main road, and does a vast trade, one of its main attractions being an impressive buffet and cold stand. Although it is a dazzling array of food, and improving all the time, the overall effect is somewhat dulled by the poor quality of the salads. These normally consist of the familiar trio of lettuce, cucumber and tomato, supplemented with miserable tinned macedoine, baked beans and chopped beetroot. It would also be good if they provided a selection of pickles and chutneys like the old nineteenth-century inns did.

But these are small matters, especially when I see what they do offer: huge pasties, the biggest I have seen outside Cornwall, lobsters that look safe, smoked trout and strips of smoked eel, rare roast beef, pâté, crab. The improvements would need time, effort, imagination, extra help and initially at least they are a gamble against familiarity and recognition. There's too much playing safe about English eating habits.

Saturday 14 April. Faggots were one of my favourite foods as a schoolboy; in those days I recall they were always known as 'savoury ducks' and were covered in a fatty membrane that had to be peeled off before the faggot was revealed. They were large, uneven-looking objects that could be bought for a few pence from any butcher's shop.

Today we had faggots for supper. They are now usually sold in foil trays of six, they are a regular size, a healthy brown colour (not the sinister offal-grey of the 'duck'), and are glued together by a thin film of insipid jelly. I had my faggots cold with processed peas; Rose wanted hers hot, so I cooked them in some of the gravy from yesterday's breast of lamb stew. The whole meal was a little too much for her.

Sunday 15 April. Early in the morning I came down to make tea; ate some of the faggot that Rose had left last night. Had the remainder for my breakfast.

Supper: I made my first Scotch eggs. The food for yesterday and today has cost less than 30p.

Wednesday 18 April. Alastair arrived. We have managed to find an outlet for his bird paintings among the flocks of tourists in Walberswick. He will be having an exhibition later in the year, but tonight there is a private view, which he is reluctant to attend, although he has dressed smartly for the occasion. A most civilized gathering, and we both drank a good deal of red wine, wisely decanted before being handed round. Some interesting morsels of food to pick at: smoked oysters, caviare, vol-au-vents made with fresh prawns. Alastair crept about nervously and was very concerned that he might have caviare in his beard.

Saturday 21 April. To Blakeney. Hannah's first long journey, her first holiday.

Monday 23 April. Rose's mother has no equal when it comes to cooking a roast, and this is part of the attraction of Blakeney; the food is always surprising, never dull or badly cooked.

Looking forward to a lunch of roast beef. Although large joints are now too costly to buy, it is still possible to have a small piece of meat cooked so that it is moist and tender. Today's little joint of topside was no exception; it had been carefully roasted, and yielded a great deal of bloody juice, which we drank by the spoonful.

Sadly returning to Suffolk tomorrow.

Wednesday 25 April. The first spring rhubarb, green and sour. I was deceived by the thickness of the stems, a common pitfall when today's fruit and vegetables are produced for their size and appearance rather than quality of taste. It simply is not true that the largest and most perfect-looking specimens have the best flavour.

Our asparagus begins to emerge.

Thursday 3 May. Things are stirring in the garden; potatoes and broad beans showing, and onions well established.

Rose planted spinach, runner beans and french beans.

Wednesday 9 May. For supper lamb stew made without onions. Rose tells me that these have risen in price to as much as 20p per pound, and some shops will not even stock them. It is easy to forget how essential they are to stews and other dishes, but we will try leeks as an alternative since they are much cheaper (8p per pound), at the moment. This is most unusual.

Wednesday 16 May. Richard here for a few days; blistering hot weather – the ground parched and starting to crack. I returned after gardening all day in the full sun and noticed that he had been collecting wild food, but I searched in vain trying to establish exactly what was planned for the meal. As I am cooking a costly

Indian meal tomorrow Richard had decided that it would be best to make do with a cheap snack. So we started with some pâté, boosted with delicious fresh, creamed horseradish. Next there were alexanders; these are the first hedgerow plant to appear after Christmas, and the stems, leaves and buds all make good eating. We had the stems, cooked like asparagus and steeped in melted butter; their delicate and aromatic flavour would convince any sceptic of the value of wild foods. Finished the meal with an omelette, speckled with chopped chives from the garden.

The evening cool and clear. This and the refreshing meal made me suggest a visit to the Bramfield Bell, where they sell the best-kept beer in the area. Before going out I prepared one of the dishes for the curry party (beef *dhansak* – a thick, rich dish that relies on the combination of lentils and lemon juice), while Richard ventured out to hunt for nightjars. But the evening had turned cold with a blustery wind, so he had little luck.

Drank several pints in the pub; the beer was bright and lively and slipped down easily. Disappointed to hear that they no longer make their own pickled eggs for sale – apparently there is no demand for them. Another small pleasure gone.

Thursday 17 May. The day of the curry. Back from gardening to finish the preparations. The *dhansak* had solidified overnight and looked well matured. Richard, wanting to contribute something to the meal, had made a rare dish (*kobi sabji*), a combination of cabbage with mustard seed which provided a good contrast to the *dhansak*. I still had to prepare a *ghobi bhaji* with one of the cauliflowers that our friend Rosemary seems to give us almost daily; also a cucumber *raitha* and some onion pickle. I'd thought of garnishing this with thinly sliced limes, but they had none in Southwold, so I had to be content with lemons.

No drink in the house. While the curries were cooking Richard and I went up to the Hart to procure a bottle of whisky. Could not afford malt, but bought a bottle of blended Lang's that proved very good.

The curry was eaten in almost total silence, everyone enjoying it too much to talk; only occasional grunts and sighs. I had planned the evening as an excuse for two pairs of our friends to meet – Rosemary and John, and Gordon and Elizabeth. They live only a few hundred yards away from each other out on the heath but were, until tonight, strangers. It was a pleasant encounter, not nervous or uncomfortable, and it was no doubt helped by the large quantities of food and whisky, which we drank liberally until after midnight.

Friday 18 May. Weather dismal. Richard decided to go home. The smell of liquor and sickly cigarette smoke lingering in the house and the remnants of the food still on the table where we left them last night.

Sunday 20 May. Ate the first asparagus from the garden; two weeks later than last year. The sticks still rather thin, but many more succulent ones are beginning to show through the buttercups that always invade our asparagus bed. I don't attempt to eradicate these; I believe that both wild and cultivated plants have a place in the garden. The area round our house has a feeling of organized wildness about it; dandelions and tulips grow together, hedge garlic and alexanders spread unchecked.

Thursday 24 May. Pulling leeks today; not my own but belonging in one of the gardens I manage. They were going to seed, but I felt I could not condemn the whole lot to the rubbish dump, so I took some home thinking that at least they would make soup.

No electricity. We were told that repairs had to be carried out, but would be finished by 5 o'clock. But at 7.30 there was still no power and we were getting hungry, so we decided to open an assortment of tins – at least when the power returned our meal would not take long to cook. Convenience food does have its uses on such occasions. We had luncheon meat and pease pudding and I prepared some of the leeks; these were stringy but softened after a long cooking.

Monday 4 June. Rose has started a part-time charring job at the Harbour Inn, Southwold. This is the local fishermen's pub and they often bring samples of their catch for sale to the drinkers. Rose was lucky and picked up four enormous whiting very cheaply. Whiting is a fish that loses its flavour soon after it is caught, but these bright-eyed specimens, fried gently in butter for a few minutes, were beautiful; the flesh melted in my mouth like fondant cream. I am sure this is one fish I could confidently eat raw in the Japanese style.

Thursday 7 June. Weather incredible, sweating hot with a clear blue sky. Saw the first frothy clusters of elderflowers.

Did some gardening at the White Hart and arranged my time so that I finished soon after evening opening. The sun was losing none of its power and I was badly in need of a pint. But the mild was thick and sweet and I was forced to have it tempered with lemonade. Got home feeling turbulent and queasy. It seems that the mild is especially susceptible to hot weather, so I have resolved to drink bitter for the rest of the summer.

Saturday 9 June. To Blakeney after lunch. As usual filled with anticipation about the food; tonight for supper, cold roast goose and salad. I remembered the first and only time I had eaten goose: it had been part of a boyhood Christmas day and I had gorged myself on the greasy meat at lunch. Not content with that, I had stuffed chocolates and cakes throughout the afternoon and had been violently sick upstairs.

Even after fifteen years the thought of goose still made me uneasy; I was haunted by the thought of my boyish excesses and that overpowering impression of grease. But I managed to eat today's goose confidently, and it had a whole range of flavours and textures that I didn't expect; the dark-brown flesh had an almost nutty flavour, it was hardly fatty (this goes quickly when the meat gets cold), and the skin had been smothered in salt, pepper and brown sugar – it was sweet and crisp like fragments from Pekin duck; Rose liked this even more than the meat itself.

I look forward to eating more goose tomorrow.

Sunday 10 June. Bad news in the local paper about crabs: the Norfolk fishermen are in trouble with poor harvests, high costs and no government subsidies. We passed a stall selling crabs while out driving in the afternoon and noticed that they were 25p each; this was ridiculously expensive (I remember when a huge one could be bought for less than a shilling), but Mac and I eagerly bought one each for our supper.

We were delayed by unexpected visitors and did not have a chance to eat until about 10.30, by which time we were all ravenously hungry. Mac and I retreated to the kitchen to dissect the crabs. Mac is an expert; he cracked the claws with his teeth and sucked out the flesh, while I made feeble use of civilized nutcrackers and the end of a teaspoon to dig out the meat. Although Mac's crab was missing one claw he seemed to have a vast heap of creamy-white meat on his plate which made the results of my efforts seem rather amateurish; this is a matter of skill and thoroughness, of knowing the make-up of the crab and where the flesh lurks.

I dressed my crab with pepper, mustard and a little vinegar and ate it with the leftovers from yesterday's salad. Excellent sweet meat. But I was still tempted by the thought of the goose, and made myself a large sandwich of it before going to bed.

Friday 15 June. Back home in Suffolk I made a tour of the garden: asparagus still thriving, fruit bushes doing well with the first gooseberries ready for picking, vegetables growing fast. It is gardener's weather.

Nothing planned for tonight's meal, until Rose returned from the Harbour with four filleted mackerel. I cut some asparagus and thought that we could eat this with the grilled fish. But in the afternoon I wandered out and collected the first gooseberries. At once the meal was transformed; without knowing it I had brought together the traditional combination of mackerel and gooseberries. One of the most pleasing aspects of food is the way a meal develops from a series of coincidences, materials in the right place at just the right moment. We are continually saved by such events.

I secreted myself in the kitchen and prepared the food. Rose occupied with feeding Hannah; this is a task she is fully equipped to perform, so I take charge of our meals while she is busy. I offered the mackerel proudly, well pleased with my efforts. The fish was soft and white after grilling, with none of the tough meatiness that mackerel often has, and the sharp gooseberry sauce contrasted perfectly with its strong oily flavour.

Thursday 21 June. The longest day of the year brings the first strawberries, and Rose out in the garden picking them under a blazing sun. It should be a good crop. We coated the berries with sugar and ate them with a spoon.

I always have doubts about using our crop for jam-making; I would rather eat the whole lot fresh and pick other fruit for preserving. I suppose this is sentimental affection for the fruit that grows in our garden.

Friday 22 June. Since Rose had Hannah she has had an aversion to all kinds of offal. She will neither cook nor eat it in any form although I've pleaded with her. But at last she produced a pig's kidney for my supper, after nagging requests for a bit of offal before I go to London.

Home from gardening to find the chopped kidney, mushrooms and onions fried on the stove – Rose out with the ponies. So I added a few spices, heated up the mixture and ate it with some rice. A pleasant send-off meal.

Saturday 23 June. Got a lift down to London with Gordon, and arrived in Berkhamsted about 7 in the evening. Midsummer's eve, and a picnic planned. Loaded up Richard's vehicle with a big box full of foods, and another containing six bottles of red wine, and headed for the Chilterns with Alastair, Nick, Mouse and Alan.

We found an orchid-covered hillside, a perfect spot even though the outline of a distant cement works rather spoilt the scene. This white monstrosity belched an unending stream of smoke into the clear evening sky, but we were too engrossed to let it bother us. Richard produced first a dish of prawns and mushrooms, followed by bits of airy French bread made heavy with rich chunks of pâté. The evening became more and more heady as we sat among the orchids, drinking wine and delving into pots of cheap caviare. I was also eating quantities of black olives, and I cannot now understand why I disliked them so much when I first visited Spain.

We lingered on the hillside till 10 o'clock; the sun was down and there was a coldness in the air. It had been a magical and opulent evening. Finally to the pub for a pint before they closed.

Sunday 24 June. Midsummer's day. In the afternoon we visited the 'fayre' at Puttenham, a local church-based occasion memorable only for the complete lack of activity or celebration. Weather stifling and overcast. We tried to develop our thirsts before an evening's drinking in the Crown and Sceptre.

Home at teatime and slightly refreshed by some apple juice flavoured with woodruff that Richard had been cultivating. The dry thirst still with us.

We ate up the remains of yesterday's picnic – some pâté, olives etc. and some slices of *lasschinken* which we had forgotten on that hillside. This is delicately cured loin of pork, and its saltiness was perfectly timed to reinforce our thirst before opening time.

A relentless night's drinking, all of us in various states of drunkenness by the end.

Monday 25 June. Slightly hung over, but had to travel up to London on business. For lunch I headed towards St Martin's Lane, and a small Indian restaurant where I was introduced to oriental cookery some years ago. I was thankful that it still offered a good curry at a reasonable price; I chose a *rogan ghosht* that was sharp, garlicy and aromatic. It succeeded in cooling me off in the heat of the afternoon.

When I got to Suffolk I found that Rose had lifted the first potatoes, although she had dug from the row of maincrop rather than the early Epicures. Still, the tiny red Desirées were splendid and tasted like West Indian sweet potatoes.

Tuesday 26 June. After her mistake potato-digging yesterday, Rose lifted some Epicures, which were still rather small.

Saturday 30 June. The weather still magnificently hot, but now we want rain. Our strawberries, after starting well, have not been as plentiful as last year. Many have turned mushy on the plants while others have not ripened at all.

Asked Rosemary to look after the garden while we are in Scotland. (At last the time for the holiday has arrived.) She will water the vegetables, check onions for signs of seeding and pick any currants that ripen while we are away. By the time we get back much of the produce will be ready for harvesting.

Made the journey to Blakeney. Norfolk blackberries in flower, and a great number of wild roses.

Tuesday 3 July. Roused ourselves at 4 in the morning and set off for Scotland with Rose's parents. By dawn we were in the Fens; hardly an acre not under cultivation with row upon row of luxuriant potato plants. Stopped in Grantham at 7 o'clock for much-needed coffee and sandwiches of chicken and mutton, eaten in the town's car-park. On through the Pennines. Yorkshire has a friendly ruggedness about it, and the first small peaks were a real foretaste of the grandeur to come. The landscape more powerful and impressive as we moved north. By lunchtime we were through Newcastle and into the ancient battlegrounds of Northumberland. This was bleak moorland cut by grey stone walls and dotted with isolated grim-looking farms and houses. All the buildings a dreary yellowish grey. The fact that people still live and work in this desolate country makes it somehow a disturbing, sinister place to visit.

It wasn't long before we neared the border; we rounded a corner on the brow of a hill, and there before us was Scotland. A vast, panoramic landscape. Then on through Edinburgh and up to Dollar where we had planned to stay overnight; we arrived exhausted and in need of a good meal. The menu was fairly standard, so I chose the safe combination of lentil soup and sirloin steak, and was pleasantly surprised by both. The soup was obviously home-made and was floated with thick cream, but it was followed by an unexpected but apparently compulsory fish course – fried fillets of sole. This was not so good. Hotels will use those bright orange artificial breadcrumbs which inevitably form an unpleasant shield around the delicate fish. Still I was so hungry that I ate this without complaining, but was relieved when a huge steak was eventually laid before me. A rough, irregular piece of meat with a good amount of crisp fat, served with sweet corn, tomatoes, onion rings fried in batter and fried potatoes. I was full and well satisfied after this, and felt ready for bed, but first I joined Mac in the bar and had a couple of malt whiskys.

Wednesday 4 July. Hotel breakfast should be a leisurely, civilized meal. It should take time, be free from distractions and above all it should be enjoyed because it begins the day. Porridge, kippers and cups of tea. Then off again, travelling north into the highlands. Unlike Northumberland, human beings seem out of place among these peaks.

Reached our destination – Ruthven – at teatime, and first called in to see our neighbours the Rose family, who live across the valley from our cottage. They welcomed us with cups of tea, and casually produced piles of little venison sandwiches which we soon devoured.

Our cottage is separated from the river Findhorn by meadows covered with orchids and wild pansies. It was a beautiful clear evening, so I took a walk with Rose. The river bank lined with weathered juniper bushes and wild thyme underfoot. Before long we saw a red deer on the far side of the river; it was visible briefly picking its way among the heather. A black rabbit darted across our path and hedgehogs ambled along the old track of a road that runs parallel to the river; they moved about without fear of being hit by cars as it is a road for walkers not motorists.

There are few vegetables in the highlands and most people live on a diet of meat, fish, potatoes, pulses and root crops. Looking at the land around Ruthven it is easy to understand this; the powder-dry soil has no depth and it is simply impossible to grow anything except turnips and swedes. There is also little sun, although at this time of year it does not get dark till almost midnight and is light again by 2 in the morning.

After supper we lay in bed, too excited to sleep, and waited for the evening light to fade.

Thursday 5 July. Mac cooked us breakfast; a highland mixed grill consisting of slices of black pudding, beef sausage and fruity pudding (a meatless sausage spotted with currants), which we ate with fried eggs and potatoes. Outside a buzzard hovered high above the glen.

I volunteered to chop wood in the morning, and while nosing around some outbuildings by our cottage, I found the barn used for sheep-shearing; it was full of fleece remnants, ropes, vicious shears and boxes of empty beer cans and whisky bottles – reminders of the sweat of the last shearing session. The atmosphere was ancient and untidy, but there in the middle of the barn stood the Roses' deep-freeze, a gleaming white cabinet; it was a sight as incongruous and disturbing as any surrealist landscape. And the freezer is more than a quarter of a mile from their cottage.

Our friend Marjorie arrived before lunch; she is a retired schoolmistress with boundless energy that often leaves us gasping. We had the first large meal of the holiday: a roll of beef roasted with potatoes, boiled onions and peas. I spent the afternoon by the river, watching oystercatchers streaking above the water, as Mac waded in the shallows and cast a hopeful line for trout.

The evening was clear again so we walked along the river to the ruined crofts of Shenachie. Before the clearances this valley sheltered about 400 families; now only two cottages are left.

Friday 6 July. Visited Inverness in the morning for supplies. A good covered market where we bought rolled lamb and rolled beef; the Scots seem to rely heavily on this style of meat for boiling. The stalls also displayed black puddings, strings of white, mealy puddings and gruesome pickled tongues. The fish stalls were interesting as well with hake, ling, copper-coloured Arbroath smokies tied in pairs, alongside piles of filleted fresh herrings. We bought some of these for supper. Vegetables are scarce and expensive because of the lack of locally grown produce, but shops do stock huge sacks of dried peas, lentils, beans and pearl barley, and we found some useful 7 lb bags of mixed pulse in a supermarket.

Cooked the herring suppers, for my first kitchen task of the holiday. There were so many fillets that I had to grill them in relays, and while waiting I made a mustard sauce to go with them. The whole meal – herrings, potatoes and sauce – was substantial without flamboyance or extravagance. It pleased everyone.

Saturday 7 July. Boiled mealy pudding for breakfast. This is a white pudding, rather like a meatless haggis made from suet, oatmeal and spices. I hope to take a couple of these home, as they are quite rare in England.

Sunday 8 July. Out after breakfast to gather some wild thyme for today's roast lamb. As I rubbed the leaves between my fingers, I noticed how mild the scent was compared with cultivated thyme. I picked a fine bunch of flowering stems and threaded sprigs under the string that bound the meat. Occupied most of the morning tending and basting the joint as it cooked.

The lamb was tender and juicy with a mild aromatic flavour. In fact I could have safely used much more thyme – whole bunches packed around the meat. I concocted some gravy from meat jelly (the bottom of the dripping bowl), a little tomato juice and the remains of yesterday's gravy.

After lunch we climbed one of the peaks that rise steeply from the banks of the river. This was a special trip, for at the summit is a family cairn which Rose's parents add to each year. But it has no historic significance, it is simply a reminder of our visits. So Rose and I set off with Hannah in the 'back pack'. At first Rose's parents said they were too tired for the climb, but we soon saw them treading the slopes with experienced steps and following an easy route. We were coming up the rough way, it was a windy ascent and the matted heather and pot-holes made progress slow. We rested on the way up and Rose sat among the heather to feed Hannah.

Eventually we reached the top, just in front of Rose's parents, and piled stones onto the monument. Then we trekked gallantly down the slope, back to the cottage and reviving cups of tea. No one had the energy or inclination to cook the evening meal, so we ate up the leftovers – some pork, beef and lamb with fried potatoes.

We are accumulating an impressive quantity of dripping.

Monday 9 July. For breakfast toast and dripping spiced with salt, pepper and Marmite. I dug deep into the bowl but found no jelly at the bottom; we must have used it up yesterday. But the dripping had an interesting mixture of flavours and textures; the hard, smooth, almost pure white lamb above layers of dark, grainy and much softer beef. The different layers looked like rock strata.

Our supply of wood was dwindling fast, so I collected and chopped another load during the morning.

After lunch we went out to visit some of the local historical sites: Cawdor castle; the prehistoric burial ground of Clava with its tombs like enormous air-raid shelters surrounded by a circle of massive stones; the simple gravestones in the thirteenth-century church of Barevan carved with strange symbols and Gaelic inscriptions. In the churchyard there is also a bizarre imitation stone coffin which was used as a punishment for village men who seduced young girls. This whole area has a very long history and must have contained some of the earliest Scottish settlements.

We got home quite late and had to prepare a speedy supper with 2 lbs of costly mince (44p a pound); this will have to last us two days. Barbara cooked it with carrots and onions in thick gravy and we ate vast quantities. Mac and I seem to have developed colossal appetites, but we managed to restrain ourselves and left enough mince for tomorrow. Finished the meal with a refreshing fruit salad made from grapefruit, oranges and bananas. It was especially welcome as a relief from much of the heavy food we have been eating.

Tuesday 10 July. An uneventful, lazy day. Marjorie laid a crust of pastry over the mince for our evening meal, and transformed yesterday's simple dish into a superb pie. After this we had ice-cream with a sauce that Rose made from melted raspberry jam. I had to go out to the deep-freeze to get the ice-cream and then rush back with the remainder after we had cut off half the block.
Wednesday 11 July. The weather has turned. It is dull, and there is a mist of fine rain in the air. By early evening the rain seemed to have passed, and Rose decided to go for a short walk along the banks of the river. After an hour she had not returned and the rain had started again. I was getting anxious and went out to search for her, but found nothing. Another half hour passed and still she was not home so Mac and I, by this time fearing the worst catastrophes, went out together. I covered the river bank while he tracked along the road in the car. We both shouted her name

across the deserted, rain-covered hillside but to little effect. Eventually we decided to check at our neighbour's cottage in case she was there. We arrived drenched to find her sitting by the fire, warm and dry and drinking tea. We were greatly relieved.

Thursday 12 July. Mac had put a pound of mixed pulse to soak overnight and by morning it had expanded to vast proportions. This was intended to go with a piece of rolled rib of beef, but the pulse and the meat together were too much for any of our saucepans. There were loud arguments in the kitchen, but we finally agreed to braise the meat and cook the pulse separately on the stove.

A splendid lunch: the braised beef, roast and boiled potatoes, a mountain of thick pulse and crisp cabbage. The beef was long-fibred but perfectly tender and not at all stringy. It was steeped in some delicious fatty onion juice. The weather again deteriorating, so we set out in the car after recovering from lunch to look at the sights. Had a cold tea when we got back – luncheon meat, tomatoes, cucumber, drop scones, pineapple cakes.

There was a mist of rain all evening, and the the air was thick with midges, but Mac succeeded in catching three trout.

Friday 13 July. Down to breakfast to find Mac eating his trout, lightly grilled. They looked very tempting, the flesh almost pink like salmon. He has promised me the next he catches, but these, the first of the holiday, rightly belonged on his plate.

To Inverness horse sale in the morning. After the sheer space of the Ruthven valley, the noise and activity of the auction ring were almost claustrophobic. We did not stay long, and were soon in the fish market buying another dozen herring fillets and a pair of Arbroath smokies.

The evening clear with a beautiful mellow light and very still.

Saturday 14 July. Boiled a haggis before going out for the day. Heavy rain and dark clouds; the river rising fast. We drove through the eerie wasteland around Lochindorb – the home of the legendary fourteenth-century terrorist, 'the wolf of Badenoch'. A desolate landscape of unkept roads, unfenced land with no sign of crofts, and there on a little island in the middle of the loch the deserted castle, its grey stone matching the colour of the water.

In the afternoon the weather cleared and we drove north to the coastal towns of Elgin, Buckie and Cullen through country that reminded us of Norfolk – a mixture of flat farmland with woods and undulating hills. Buckie is a working fishing town: bright boats in the harbour, all with imitation wood panels painted on their cabins; houses on the seafront built end on to break the wind from the sea; smells of kippers, stale fish and diesel oil. But we found the local fish shop disappointing with only some fresh and salted cod and herring fillets that looked old. Bought two 7 lb bags of mixed pulse to bring home with us.

When we got back to Ruthven, our plans for supper were delayed by Lewis offering to shear a few sheep for us. We had hoped to see the full shearing, but sadly the Roses were not ready. Still, Lewis demonstrated his skills impressively; he floored the sheep with the speed and strength of a performing wrestler and pared off the fleece with confident cuts of the shears, without even scratching the skin of the animal. The whole operation took him little more than two minutes. Even the way the fleece was bundled up and secured was cunning, and no task for an amateur. After watching him shear three sheep we dashed across the meadow through the sodden grass and the pouring rain, back to the cottage and supper. We began with an appetizer of cold herring left over from yesterday, eaten with sliced cucumber and mustard; then a dish of mince.

Sunday 15 July. For breakfast, haggis sliced and fried with potatoes. Quite different to the variety we buy in Suffolk; much less spicy and altogether less heavy on the stomach.

Monday 16 July. Began the day with an Arbroath smokie, which I split, stuffed with butter and warmed under the grill. It had a delicate flavour, even milder than Finnan haddock, and the flesh was still almost white. I ate the skin which was crisp and sweet. But I must have eaten the fish far too quickly, for later in the morning I was taken with a severe bout of indigestion.

After lunch I felt much better, and we all went out in the car. It was about 5 o'clock when we stopped in a lonely valley to have a cup of tea. Mac with his sharp eyesight was first to spot a moving speck high up in the sky. It was a golden eagle, a young one, easily visible with binoculars as it wheeled over the peaks. A magnificent sight. When it moved out of view we continued on our way home, but had to stop again because I saw a red deer stalking among the rowan trees and bracken near the side of the road. We watched it until it sensed our presence and vanished silently into the undergrowth.

Later we talked about the eagle and the deer as we ate blocks of rum and raisin fudge bought in a roadside shop.

Tuesday 17 July. Our last day at the cottage. Again the weather dull and rainy. Marjorie left, to make her way back to Norfolk by coach and train, and we consoled ourselves with a final meal of boiled mutton and pulse. Both Mac and I agreed that we would rather eat good mutton than beef.

Occupied most of the day in getting ready for an early start in the morning.

Wednesday 18 July. After saying our farewells to the Roses, we headed south and homeward. At first I was preoccupied with memories of the holiday, the foods we had discovered – venison, mutton, mealy puddings, Arbroath smokies and the pulse; and I remembered too the sight of golden eagles, buzzards and deer, and casual curlews wandering along the road in front of our car; then more generally I thought of what we had seen of the highlands themselves, their powerful and eerie history and the scars left by the clearances.

But before long my thoughts were turning to Suffolk and our cottage; I was anxious to see how my vegetables had grown during our absence, especially the onions and french beans.

We were staying overnight in the border town of Kelso, and without knowing it we had arrived during the celebrations of 'beating the bounds', and the evening before the Kelso ride. And we were in the hotel that was the centre of the festivities. The men were drinking whisky washed down with beer, and eating greasy fish and chips from newspaper. They made a great deal of noise.

Thursday 19 July. Watched the beginning of the ride before we resumed our journey home. Originally these rides were ways of defining territorial limits, but now the occasion is little more than an excuse for dressing up and riding horses which are often completely out of condition. We saw them set off in drizzling rain; there must have been a hundred or more, with riders who were still feeling the effects of last night's drink, sitting askew in the saddle, bouncing ridiculously and hanging onto the reins in desperation, for fear of falling off.

After they had left the town we started on the last stage of our journey. Eventually we arrived home in the early evening; although the East Anglian sky was clear and pale blue, there must have been some bad weather, for the ripe cornfields had been flattened by severe gales and rain.

We were hungry when we got back, so Barbara found numerous tins of beans, potatoes and frankfurter sausages which

I duly opened and heated up. The food tasted delicious. Over a glass of whisky Rose and I thanked Mac for the holiday, and for his safe and expert driving.

Friday 20 July. Rose, Hannah and I travelled back to Suffolk. Had a look at the garden and was pleased to find fat onions, not gone to seed, french beans ready to pick, and runner beans in flower. But the black fly has ruined our crop of broad beans.

Monday 23 July. Picked the first of the french beans. They were very young, pale green pods, pencil-thin without bulges from the swollen seeds. I cooked them whole with freshly dug Epicures boiled with a couple of leaves of applemint, and served them with some pig's liver fried with slices of bacon so that the flavours mingled.

One of the greatest pleasures of home cooking when I was a boy was to help with the liver and bacon. I used to volunteer to stir the gravy simply to taste the blobs of congealed blood that exuded from the meat during the frying and stuck to the bottom of the pan. As I stirred, I would dig around to find these treasured morsels, and would spoon them out when no one was watching.

Thursday 26 July. Huge ripe blackberries seen along the road to Sibton Green. It will be a good season for these and other hedge-row fruit.

Friday 27 July. Rose and I invited to Gordon's house for supper; a shoulder of lamb roasted and eaten with spinach and potatoes. These were sliced layer by layer with onions, and cooked in milk in the oven. Elizabeth also made some onion sauce – the best I have ever tasted; it was thick and creamy with good chunks of solid onion.

Gordon pointed out that we were in fact eating a high-class version of Lancashire hot-pot, a dish he knew well from his childhood in the North of England. The important fact was that in the original hot-pot the ingredients – lamb, onions, potatoes and vegetables – were cooked together, but here they were served as separate dishes. Poor people tended to cook all their food together in stews, soups, etc. to save on fuel, time and money. Others, who could afford these things, would lay out their food on the table as individual dishes.

Sunday 29 July. Rose cooked a gooseberry crumble. But I was surprised when I cut it open, for fumes of orange poured out. She had chopped up one orange and put it to cook among the gooseberries. It was a marvellous, simple stroke to contrast the smooth mushy gooseberry with the sharp flavour of the orange.

Thursday 2 August. The countryside is suddenly alive with fungi. I have seen at least ten edible species over the past week – puffballs, parasols, champignons, ceps, horse mushrooms and many

others. Their size and profusion are extraordinary, although the climate has been ideal: a long, hot spell and then rain.

Gathered the first giant puffball of the year. I picked it from a shady roadside bank and, balancing it dangerously in one hand, cycled home. Odd looks from the villagers as I paraded this white sphere along the street. I cooked some of it for my supper; I simply sliced it and fried it in butter. It tasted like marshmallow, although the skin was slightly bitter and should really have been peeled off first.

After supper I picked some more french beans and the first runner beans. Took some up to Gordon with a chunk of puffball, which he cooked straight away. He mixed it with cream and butter and heaped it onto pieces of toast. He was astonished by its taste.

Monday 6 August. Have been on my own over the weekend; Rose in Blakeney for a few days with Hannah. Out in the morning to lift my onions and to pick another huge basketful of french beans.

Very little in the larder, so I decided to make up a kind of vegetable *bhaji* with onions, french beans and a young marrow that I cut prematurely from our luxuriant marrow bed. The dish was hot and spicy, and I cooled myself with a large mugful of milk afterwards.

Wednesday 8 August. Richard, Mouse and Alan here for a few days. Hope to have some interesting foods and good drinking sessions while they are here.

Thursday 9 August. I was out gardening all day, while Richard went in search of fungi. Back to find that he had picked two of the biggest puffballs I had ever seen; one weighed well over 5 lbs. We all posed on the lawn like soccer-players with the fungi between our knees while photographs were taken.

Richard wanted to stuff the puffballs and bake them in the oven. This was a monumental task. We had to hollow out the flesh of the larger puffball and mix it with mince, chopped onion and herbs. Then we spooned this into the puffball, put it in a dish, covered it in foil and slid it carefully into the oven. We changed our minds about the other puffball, cut it into thick slices and laid pieces of bacon between them. We had fears that the puffballs might soak up fat, or shrink and dry out during cooking, but neither of these disasters occurred. The puffballs had made some moist juice and had absorbed some fat and liquid, but they were still white and meaty; we carved them like poultry. These two monster dishes were far too much, even for five of us, for puffballs are the richest of all fungi and simply cannot be eaten in large quantities safely, especially before an evening's drinking.

While we were eating, a young boy from the village called and wanted Richard to identify a fungus related to the field mushroom. Richard was suitably impressive.

We all visited the Bramfield Bell after supper, drank quantities of bitter and played long games of darts.

Friday 10 August. Met Richard, Mouse and Alan in the White Hart for lunch after a morning's gardening. Richard treated us. We shared some smoked herring fillets and smoked trout; an interesting contrast that showed just how much variety there can be in smoked fish. The herrings were dark brown, coarse and very salty, while the trout was delicate with a mild smoky flavour. But it was a pity that the indifferent salad didn't match the superb qualities of the fish.

Tuesday 14 August. The rowan trees are covered with ripe berries, but the birds have started to devour them, and there will be few left in two weeks' time. Made rowan jelly.

Thursday 16 August. There is a glut of tomatoes; they can now be bought for 5p a pound and are the cheapest I can remember. It is a real treat to be able to use fresh tomatoes regardless of cost. One of my favourite uses is in sandwiches, and I took a batch with me for my lunch while gardening. While these are good when freshly made, they improve after the juice has had time to soak into the bread and stain it pink.

Today the hottest day of the year – a temperature of 95°F recorded in Bury St Edmunds – but the first leaves are already beginning to fall.

Friday 17 August. Felt bad all day from the effects of yesterday's sun.

Sunday 19 August. Tried the first of the rowan jelly with a piece of stuffed breast of lamb. I am very pleased with it; the characteristic smoky aroma is there and the jelly is a beautiful wine-red colour with a slightly bitter flavour. It suited the strong flavour of the lamb, although it would probably be less successful with other cuts such as leg or shoulder which are altogether sweeter and milder in flavour. I want to try it with some other kinds of meat.

Monday 27 August. We have found a local farm and nursery where we can buy tomatoes for 2½p a pound; they also sell aubergines, green and red peppers, chillies and fruit. Rose went over there and came back with a large box of assorted vegetables.

The tomatoes were very ripe and needed to be used up quickly, so we decided to make chutney and include some chopped exotic vegetables with the more usual ingredients. Rose had never experienced the sensation of raw chilli, so I cut one open and told her to put the tip of her tongue to it. She did so, and recoiled, her mouth burning. So to make the chutney palatable I had to cut out the central core and scrape out the seeds of the chillies I was intending to use. We made a large panful of chutney, enough to fill six jars. It was a dazzling sight – the bright red tomatoes with the green of the peppers and the purple of the aubergine skins.

It is a luxury to have such a cheap supply of unusual vegetables, and we now chop them up and throw them into almost any dish that we are making. They can transform the dullest of meals.

Thursday 30 August. The supply of exotic vegetables continues to solve many of our food problems. We concocted an unusual supper from the only ingredients we had in the house – exotic and garden vegetables, rice and bacon. Cooked one of our marrows and put it chopped into a cheese sauce with pieces of bacon. Then I made a dish of fried vegetables with peppers, tomatoes, onions, potatoes, and courgettes and runner beans left over from yesterday. The two dishes were piled alongside one another on a mound of boiled rice. In fact each one would have made a complete meal on its own.

Sunday 2 September. Picked the first of the violet-podded french beans; in fact they are dark purple but when cut open they reveal green flesh and tiny white seeds. It was fascinating to watch them turning from purple to dark green as they cooked. I ate them with thick lamb chops (mahogany brown on the outside, pink and moist inside), Desirée potatoes and marrow.

Thursday 6 September. There seems to be no let-up in the hot weather. I again sweated while gardening all day, but at the end of the afternoon a cooling breeze and the gift of a bunch of grapes offered some relief from the heat. I had intended to take the grapes home for Rose, but could not resist tasting them first. They were sublime thirst-quenchers, green and muscat-scented. After the rigours of digging and hedge-cutting, a mouthful of sweet grapes was reward enough.

Sunday 9 September. Alastair arrived for his exhibition next week in Walberswick. He looked shattered after a freezing drive in his outrageous ex-army jeep; he was ragged, nervous and confused. He brought us presents wrapped in a voluminous green curtain; a loaf of home-made bread, shaped like a brick and with a delicious wheaty smell, also two bottles of wine – one an ordinary white, the other a vintage home-brewed rhubarb dating from 1964.

Both he and I were in the mood for a drink, so we made our way up to the White Hart, Alastair obviously relishing the thought of driving me there. It was a daring, exhilarating ride. Marvellous clear Broadsides in the pub; they were still strong, but tasting more refined than the early brews.

Poor Rose, back at home ironing while we drank.

Monday 10 September. I have often tried to convince Rose of her abilities as a cook, yet she still seems to do herself an injustice by maintaining that she can cook little more than basic food. But tonight's meal proved my point; it was lamb's kidneys cooked slowly with onions, tomatoes and herbs. The kidneys had steeped in the tomato juice and looked pink and succulent. Each half had curled into a ball, inviting a stab of the fork and into the mouth whole. She served these with some enormous sticks of macaroni which looked like long pasta drainpipes; Alastair enjoyed playing tricks with these, sucking and blowing into them, and twisting them into grotesque and lurid shapes.

Thursday 13 September. We were expecting Richard to come up this weekend, and had planned a visit to the Oysterage and a curry. But Alastair and he seemed hardly on good terms and had created a load of complications and problems. So Alastair, becoming more and more depressed, decided to go home, and it seemed unlikely that Richard would now visit us. We had some farewell pints in the White Hart, and afterwards I insisted that we drink the rhubarb wine. I heaved out the cork and immediately noticed a distinct smell of sherry, an impression reinforced by the colour of the wine. Curiously enough it tasted rather like a dry sherry, but lacked the sensation that comes from the evaporation of the liquor in one's mouth; this wine had no vapour. But for a home brew it was convincing, interesting, and it mellowed both of us considerably; by the end of the evening we were in good spirits.

Alastair remembered the story of this wine, how as a spindly schoolboy he had been given the job of going into the garden to pick the rhubarb after his father had announced that there would be wine-making. Alastair prepared the wine and the following year his father bottled it. Apparently there are only four bottles of this brew remaining.

Saturday 15 September. Spent much of the afternoon on the phone to Richard, trying to establish whether he was coming up to Suffolk or not. Finally he decided against it; he was sulking and I was annoyed. In all it had been a doomed week, but I was determined that the weekend at least should not be ruined. So I rang Rosemary and John and invited them to the Oysterage, and then I rang Gordon and arranged for him to come and have a curry with us tomorrow night. I felt much better and the prospects for the weekend looked good.

The Oysterage is a marvellous little place, laid out like a French café; a small, light room packed with bare wooden tables. The window space is lined with smoked fish, and the cooking is done on a small four-ring cooker in one corner of the restaurant. And you can watch the lady proprietor carving smoked salmon into transparent paper-thin slices, with the skill of a surgeon.

The secret of eating here is not to plan a meal in courses, but to order each item as you feel like it. There are no vegetables or trimmings except brown bread, toast and so on. I remember one occasion when I introduced Mac to the restaurant; he immediately grasped the spirit of the place, and after four different items, including a dessert, he suddenly ordered a plate of jellied eels. It was a gesture worthy of applause.

Tonight I had smoked sprats with an unidentifiable brown relish that was sweet and fiery but went well with the oily fish.

Then some smoked eel on toast; not the usual dry strips, but fat, creamy pieces looking more like rock salmon. They were moist, chunky and very rich; they needed lemon juice. As usual I drank Portuguese white wine with the fish. John had oysters – the main feature of the restaurant along with smoked salmon – but I must admit that I find them unpleasant. They have an odd, almost metallic aftertaste and their glutinous texture is too much for me. I finished my meal with a fresh salmon mousse, salad and some fine mayonnaise.

Sunday 16 September. Preparations for the curry occupied me for most of the day, but by the evening everything was ready. Gave Gordon prawn *dhansak* and a potato curry (*aloo bhaji*) served on a bed of spinach. I had told him that it would be a mere snack, a light meal, but on reflection the quantity of food was staggering, yet we managed to get it all eaten.

Monday 17 September. Exhausted by the weekend's eating. Rose found a bargain in the supermarket, tinned salmon roes. These odd-looking pink objects were coiled like embryos around one another in the tin. Although they looked coarse and grainy they were in fact soft-textured, but meaty as well. We rolled them in flour, fried them and ate them with hot buttered toast. A snack of a meal, but worth the eating.

Friday 21 September. A sudden turn in the weather; no more bright autumn days for a while, I fear. The afternoon bitterly cold, raining fast and with a threat of fog. We lit the first fire of the season. The change in the weather has caught us unprepared;

we must now think about stocks of food and fuel to sustain us over the coming months.

Thursday 27 September. Since we came back from Scotland we have been looking for a cottage, and at last it seems that we have found one. It is in Bramfield, and we can rent it from next month.

The first job was to harvest what was ready in our garden, particularly the marrows. I made several journeys between the garden and kitchen with armfuls of these heavy vegetables. At the moment they are piled neatly in one corner of the kitchen, a huge mass of green and yellow objects. I hope to make marrow jam, marrow rum and marrow mangoes, but the move will probably disrupt our activities so that we will get very little done.

In the evening Rose and I went over to Bramfield to see the cottage and meet the owner. He is an American and always keeps a stock of bourbon in the house, so I found myself drinking several large glasses of this very quickly. Rather unsteady on my feet when I got home. Even Rose, usually sober, has taken to wine-drinking.

Friday 28 September. It was a happy coincidence that Rosemary should invite us for supper tonight; a good opportunity to celebrate the fact that we have found somewhere to live. Gordon and Elizabeth joined us, bringing a bottle of sherry as their contribution to the occasion.

Rosemary had obviously taken great trouble to ensure that this was a real celebration, and she masterminded the evening with care, grace and elegance. None of us was allowed to notice the problems of the kitchen as we sat round the oblong wooden table lit by candles, and waited for the first course. We began with pancakes stuffed with prawns and haddock in a sauce; Gordon, always ready to translate a dish into its French equivalent, quickly identified this as a variant of *crêpe de fruits de mer*. It was served in lovely earthenware dishes. Then John went into the kitchen and carved thick chunks of lamb from a whole leg roasted with garlic and rosemary; the vapours set us sniffing in anticipation. Such quantities of lean meat were startling; Rose and I simply cannot afford to eat with such lavishness normally. So meals like this become even more special as increasing food prices dictate what we can realistically eat.

This large, heavy course was balanced by a feather-light lemon mousse, and by some of the ripest cheese I had ever eaten; brie that seemed to spread over the plate like thick cream, and gorgonzola with that characteristic burning taste.

The meal could hardly have been improved and we collapsed into armchairs after it, to talk and drink coffee. It was exactly the sort of occasion that Rose and I needed after nervous months of house-hunting; a fine meal, a chance to relax. We did not leave until the early hours of the morning.

Saturday 29 September. Over to Southwold in the afternoon to do some shopping. I wanted to make a stuffed marrow, to use up one of our crop, and I decided that liver would be an appropriate filling.

At home I set to work and peeled one of the largest specimens and cut it into thick rings. Rather than bake the marrow whole in the oven, I intended to make a quick version of the dish. I fried the liver, chopped and mixed it with tomatoes, green peppers, garlic and onions. Then I boiled the marrow rings. Unfortunately

I was sidetracked by a programme on the radio and the marrow overcooked; as a result the rings began to fall apart. But I managed to piece them together in the frying pan, stuffed them with the liver mixture, and fried them. I did not dare turn them in case they disintegrated, so I cooked them on one side only and then carefully lifted the pieces out of the pan onto our plates. The meal was saved.

Saturday 6 October. Up to Blakeney for the weekend. Mac had secured the carcasses of a ewe and a lamb for his deep-freeze, and was busy in the afternoon, butchering them and packing them for the freezer. He divided the carcasses, working away with knife and saw, and packed up chops and pieces for boiling and roasting. He laid aside the kidneys for tomorrow's breakfast.

Sunday 7 October. Mac cooked the kidneys, which we ate with fatty fried potatoes. The two I had were enormous, and although one was from the ewe and the other from the lamb, I could detect no difference in appearance or taste.

I rarely eat kidneys for breakfast nowadays, but it was not always so. I remember my father bringing them home regularly when I was a boy. In fact my breakfast eating habits then were almost Victorian: as well as kidneys and massive fried breakfasts, I had a passion for cold curry, and Finnan haddock steamed in milk and butter.

Rose and I returned to Suffolk in the afternoon, taking with us two joints of mutton to store in Rosemary's freezer. The joints had a curious smell of new meat about them, and their flesh was bright red with solid white fat around it.

Tuesday 9 October. As we are packing up the contents of our cottage, there is less facility for cooking and preparing food; it is becoming an increasingly chancy process. Lack of tools makes cooking even the simplest foods a daunting project.

Still Richard and Fran were here for a couple of days, and decided to see what they could make of some whiting fillets. They produced a sensibly planned and confidently prepared meal: Richard put together a salad of watercress, almonds and oranges – a marvellous dish to look at. The main course was grilled whiting with solid bright orange carrots and young marrow that was greenish in colour. In fact this course echoed the salad exactly in terms of its different colours. Fran made a good sauce for the fish: a bechamel decorated with fennel and flavoured with cheese and lemon juice. It was thick and yellow but did not overpower the fish.

Out drinking afterwards. The fennel taste remained and was intensified by the beer; a constant reminder of the meal.

Friday 12 October. Over the past few days we have been forced to live on tinned food and sausages. The kitchen is now clear and we are almost ready to move.

Sunday 14 October. The house is bare. We seem to have almost completely abandoned cooking; the prospect is too dismal. The kitchen is empty and the sitting-room has been cleared except for two armchairs and a carpet. Most of the weekend spent in moving furniture, so we had even less time for food.

But there was a tin of cod's roe in the house, so I made a kind of mock caviare by mixing it with lemon juice and cayenne pepper.

We spread the caviare onto pieces of toast as we sat round the fire in our chairs. Such simple foods have the habit of restoring spirits at the right moment, and we were soon cheerful again.

Monday 15 October. We made evening toast by a warm fire. The crisp slices smelled of smoke, and once we had started eating it was difficult to stop; the easy ritual of the fork held in the grate and the spreading of warm butter was far too tempting.

Thursday 18 October. The coming of autumn. The season has changed almost in the space of one day, and there is now a coldness in the air. Clay fields, polished by the cut of the plough, shining like bronze in the sunlight; the clods rest heavily on one another. But there is honeysuckle in flower and the brambles are still laden with fruit. Pheasants and rabbits dart from these growing hedgerows while broken and leafless trees lean with the wind. It is a season of contrasts and contradictions.

The sugar-beet harvest is under way and everywhere there are convoys of heavy lorries – as sure a sign of the season as any bird migration.

For us this is a time of settling in, a preparation for the struggles and problems of winter.

Saturday 20 October. Finally moved to the new cottage in Bramfield. My first impressions were of a working village, much more of a close-knit community than Wenhaston. It's a village with a centre – a large thatched 'bus shelter', although no buses stop there. The shelter stands at the crossroads, and our cottage is situated at one corner, opposite a pub and the village shop; this has more of the character of a supermarket, and sells everything from vegetables to mountaineering boots.

The pub opposite the cottage only sells gassy keg beer and lager, so we are unlikely to drink there, particularly as the delights of the Bell are so near. It also seems to be a meeting-place for leather-jacketed motor cyclists on Friday and Saturday nights; the thunderous sound of bikes is one rather annoying feature of the village.

The cottage itself is rather smaller than the Wenhaston house, with iron trellis-work covered with tangled roses. The garden is over-stocked with a random selection of plants; great numbers of evening primroses still in flower. At the moment there is little space for vegetables. From my study window I can look across the road to the church; a sturdy rustic building without a steeple, but with a separate and much older tower that attracts many amateur photographers. And at the top of our garden is the curved 'crinkly-crankly' wall that marks the boundary of the Hall.

Sunday 21 October. I was eager to start cooking in our new kitchen, but before beginning I had to find out exactly what was in the house: a jar of Hellman's mayonnaise in the fridge and a tin of salmon in the larder. Outside in the garden I discovered a bed of huge-leaved spinach, which I had already seen from a distance, but thought that Bill was cultivating horseradish as the leaves were of that proportion – growing stout, upright and bright green.

Some months ago Richard remarked that meals are often what you can 'grub together', and this was no exception. It was basically a question of making the best use of what ingredients I had found; altogether different to the cooking of a meal planned in advance, when the ingredients are collected together specifically for one dish.

So, to work: first I mashed up the salmon with some mayonnaise, lemon juice and black pepper. I put this into a dish and covered it with grated cheese and brown breadcrumbs, and warmed it under the grill while I cooked the spinach. The marvellous thing about the dish was the crust formed by the breadcrumbs, which succeeded in keeping the salmon mixture moist and creamy. I served up the salmon, crust uppermost on a bed of buttered spinach. The two really had to be eaten together for the full effect; the creamy liquor drained from the salmon and mixed with the melted butter of the spinach.

Monday 22 October. It is cold weather again, and this means hot, filling breakfasts. The season makes demands and eating habits have to change to cope with the freezing, bed-lingering mornings. When this happens we take out the porridge.

Wednesday 24 October. The monster bag of mixed pulse that we brought back from Scotland and stored in a gallon glass jar will now have its uses; like porridge it is a weighty food for winter.

Soaked a couple of handfuls overnight to go with some scrag end of lamb to make a thick stew. When we had eaten the meat and chunks of swede and parsnip, we cooked up the remains and finished off the evening with some true Scotch broth.

Tuesday 30 October. Rode to Southwold to see if there was anything interesting in the fish shops. Spotted a tray of 'golden' red herrings and eagerly bought one. Local fish-curers are once again producing quantities of these very salty fish, which are ideal for provoking a thirst.

Had the herring cold for my supper; I simply split it open and flavoured it with a little lemon juice and cayenne pepper. It was not as dry or unpleasantly salty as I had been led to believe, but it did bring on a craving for drink. I should have gone to the Bell for a pint, but lazily settled for a cup of coffee. This did little to cure my thirst.

Wednesday 31 October. An astonishing day. The weather has turned again to summer. Hot, a dazzling clear blue sky and the trees looking luxuriant and green. Such days seem peculiar to this part of East Anglia.

Thursday 1 November. We try to make pickled onions each year, and normally grow shallots specifically for that purpose. But this year we lapsed and did not plant any, so Rose had to buy several pounds for pickling.

I am always banished to the far corners of the house when peeling shallots or onions, and I spent much of the evening alone, busily peeling and putting the shallots into brine. I had to wipe the tears from my eyes often, and after dealing with three pounds my thumb was sore and grazed from the pressure of the knife. It is a slow and painstaking process since carefree use of the knife results in browning when the shallots are put into vinegar.

Friday 2 November. After the shallots had stood overnight in brine, I packed them into the gallon salad-cream jar that we always use for this pickle.

Saturday 3 November. Rose has been collecting some enormous windfall apples; perfect for baking with brown sugar and raisins. We have given pounds away to friends, stored others in trays and made some apple pulp for storing in Rosemary's freezer.

Monday 5 November. Had another red herring. This time I wanted to see if it was successful grilled like a kipper and then spread with butter. I much preferred it eaten cold.

Wednesday 7 November. Richard arrived in the evening, quite late, but still in time for us to visit the Bell for three pints. I had almost forgotten the excellence of the place and how well they keep the beer. It is always served up in straight glasses and for some reason it seems to slip down more easily from these. In the pub the old men were sitting at their table as before, playing dominoes and drinking odd mixtures of beer and sherry.

It's a real blessing to have a pub within walking distance; too often we have to drive miles for a decent pint.

Thursday 8 November. After breakfast we organized ourselves for a trip to Berkhamsted with Richard. A chance for my mother to see Hannah – in fact this will be only our second visit since she was born. She sat in her seat at the back of the car, very patient and uncomplaining for most of the journey. We stopped at lunchtime for a pint and something to eat, and found ourselves drinking a most unpleasant beer, little more than flavoured water. Fortunately I had only ordered a cautious half, while Richard struggled in vain with the contents of a pint glass. We left quickly, hoping to find another pub with a more palatable brew, and were soon outside a Greene King house. We drank some decent draught bitter, and Richard, who now seems to have an obsessive interest in beers and breweries, bought samples of all their bottled beers for a tasting session when we got to Berkhamsted.

Arrived in the middle of the afternoon and after recovering from the journey I decided to have a walk in the town. In the local delicatessen I found some *gaffelbitar* (herring tit-bits) and bought a can; I worked out what to do with them while wandering home in the dark. Eventually I made a salad with the fish, chopped apple and chopped onion, moistened with some of the liquor from the can and a little tarragon vinegar. While this was getting cool in the larder, Richard and I sat down to test the beers. A good selection, ranging from light ales like Spanish *cerveza* to dark strong ales like the Broadside.

Had the *gaffelbitar* salad before our evening meal, while finishing off the light beers. *Gaffelbitar* are herrings pickled in a mixture of vinegar, sugar and spices usually with hops and sandalwood to colour the flesh pink. The fillets are cut into thin slices before packing. The fish is completely transformed by the pickling process and tastes more like an exotic raw ham than any sort of herring.

Friday 9 November. Richard wanted to take me out to lunch at one of the local hotels where they sell a kind of *ceviche* – mackerel marinaded in lemon juice with nutmeg. I would have liked to go, but as Rose was spending the day in London, I had to stay in and look after Hannah.

Rose arrived back in the evening very merry.

Saturday 10 November. Felt very low in the morning with a bad cold. Stayed in bed till after lunch, and then struggled up to watch a rugby international on television and to help Richard in the kitchen, as he was holding an informal dinner party in the evening, a kind of Middle Eastern buffet.

A fast and exciting match, but Richard missed most of it, as he was occupied with a mammoth telephone call; in fact he spent so much time on the phone that we had to rush the meal together in under two hours. He was planning three main dishes, and the kitchen table was overflowing with ingredients. First an *eggah* – a kind of heavy egg custard – bulked out in this case with chopped leeks and spring onions. This presented few problems; I peeled and chopped the vegetables while Richard cracked and whisked numerous eggs.

The major difficulties arose when we began the *hummus*. For a start Richard had been unable to get any chick-peas and we were forced to improvise with two varieties of dried beans. These had little time to soak and even less time to cook; so they could not be ground to a paste. The beans simply would not pass through a sieve, and the liquidizer made little impression on them. We had to abandon the *hummus* and serve the beans whole as a salad decorated with radishes and chopped red peppers.

By this time Richard was beginning to panic; time was short and we still had one more dish to prepare. He cooked up some meat-balls and artichoke hearts, while I was given the task of dealing with some cans of vacuum-packed bread dough. (The bread situation rather hopeless in Berkhamsted.) The cans were made of stiffened card with metal end-pieces, and had to be opened by giving them a violent blow rather like cracking an egg. A loud explosion, the cardboard unwrapped itself and the dough seeped out. I put pieces to bake in the oven.

At last the meal was ready, friends began to arrive and Richard and I paced about nervously, drinking glasses of Moroccan red wine. Richard drank very fast and heavily, obviously worried about the food and determined to survive the evening with a show of exuberance and merriment. But it was an awkward and witless gathering, and the food did little to save the occasion. I was saddened and irritated by the whole spectacle, especially as I was involved and partly responsible for the unsuccessful food. But had we been in better spirits we could have accepted these shortcomings; as it was, the evening turned sour.

Thursday 15 November. Now that we are settled in our cottage, we have time to make preserves again. Some of the marrows that we had transported from Wenhaston were getting old and yellow so we had to use them up. Tried various recipes for marrow jam, none of which was entirely right. I think that the marrows were too old; they remained stringy and did not soften or blend well in the jam. Still the results may turn out to be useful as fillings for tarts.

Friday 16 November. Rose went to help out at a dinner arranged for the local old people, and returned with some excellent left-overs – slices of cold roast beef and hunks of strong home-made cheddar cheese. I thought the beef had been seasoned with black pepper until Rose told me that she had dropped the valuable slices onto the road as she got out of the car; they were speckled with dirt and bits of grit. Still, after scraping as much as possible from the meat, we ate it in sandwiches, and reluctantly saved some for tomorrow to eat with pickles.

Saturday 17 November. Rose not feeling well. She stayed in bed for most of the day, I waited on her and coped with Hannah. Plenty of vegetables in the house, so I made a thick soup which I thought might improve Rose's condition. There was still fresh fennel in the garden, and I picked a few sprigs with some fresh sage and thyme to put into the soup. While working with the herbs, I thought I would try drying some of the sage, and also some mint and the bay leaves that we had cut from the important tree at our Wenhaston cottage. Although November is hardly the best time for drying herbs, the morning was bright and dry and the plants were still in good condition. I tied the leafy twigs in bundles and hung them from the oak beam in our sitting-room.

Sunday 18 November. Rose much better, and her parents visiting us for the day. Lunch – a piece of mutton roasted. I wanted to spend time on this meal, and try out some basting with a liquor made from orange juice, mustard and melted redcurrant jelly. I nursed the joint as it cooked, basting and turning it from time to time, and carried on my solitary tasks even after Rose's parents arrived. Then Mac suggested a quick lunchtime pint and I left the meat, confident that it would not be ruined by lack of attention.

Once in the Bell we settled down to some drinking, and discovered a rare malt whisky behind the bar. This detained us, for we were determined to sample this dark malt, and by the time we left the pub we were quite merry, and I had almost forgotten the meal. Fortunately Rose had got the joint out of the oven before it spoiled completely, but even so it was crusted with a layer of burnt sugar. I bravely cut this away – only the outer fat was affected – and sliced the meat. The crust must have protected the meat for it was beautifully moist and tender, and sweetened by the basting. We ate the whole meal greedily, and there was really nothing wrong with the food, although Rose scorned me cruelly for my mistakes.

Before Rose's parents went home they left another piece of mutton for us.

Monday 19 November. I suggested that Rose should trim the fat from the large shoulder of mutton that her parents left with us yesterday, and render it down for dripping, before boiling the joint.

I came back from gardening to find the meat nearly cooked, so my task – a favourite one – was to make the caper sauce. It was a marvellous piece of meat, and reminded me of the venison we had eaten in Scotland; it had the same dark, fibrous quality and an equally strong flavour.

Tuesday 20 November. Rose used up the remains of the mutton cooked with apples and green grapes.

Saturday 24 November. A dismal evening and very little in the larder. Rose baked some potatoes in their jackets, and when these were cooked she scooped out the insides and mixed in some grated cheese and chopped fried bacon. After refilling the skins she browned the potatoes under the grill. Between us we ate six potatoes.

There are signs of an imminent fuel crisis in the land.

Monday 26 November. Hannah is growing fast, and now likes scrambled egg for her breakfast.

Tuesday 27 November. Visited Norwich to do some work in the library. At lunchtime Rose's mother appeared unexpectedly and took me to the Assembly Rooms for a meal. The building is used for civic functions and exhibitions and it has a palatial air; rooms with high ceilings, decorated with paintings and chandeliers – a place to wander about in. The restaurant itself is a huge long room packed with little round tables and a cold stand that stretches its whole length. An enormous selection of cold and hot food.

I chose what I wanted very carefully, determined to have a leisurely meal and to exert some self-control over the quantities of food that I ate. It was a great temptation to order extravagantly, but I managed to restrain myself and had some pâté with tomatoes, a little cole slaw salad and some French bread.

Over a glass of lemon tea we discussed plans for Christmas. Rose and I hope to go up to Blakeney again.

Wednesday 28 November. It snowed heavily in the evening and by the time we went to bed the ground was covered. Out of curiosity I stuck a ruler in the snow; it was already more than two inches deep.

There are signs that we may be in for a bad winter; power cuts, fuel shortages and the possibility of a dearth of basic supplies could lead to a real struggle for survival, particularly if the weather is harsh. We may need all our resourcefulness and imagination to keep going.

Saturday 1 December. Rose was busy in the evening making some fudge, flavoured with small cubes of crystallized ginger. Her fudge is always rather soft, not at all like the rock-hard blocks of candy that shops tend to sell. The recipe she uses is a simple one, and she manages without the aid of thermometers and clocks. It was an excellent batch and we ate nearly all of it before going to bed.

Friday 7 December. I had to make supper from a quarter of a pound of mince, and decided to bulk the meat out with potato and onions and flavour the mixture with sage, to make tiny spherical rissoles. I thought that I would try deep-frying them in the chip pan; this was successful but I had to watch the rissoles carefully to ensure that they didn't overcook and finish up like lumps of coke.

Saturday 8 December. Rose made her Christmas cake. It was constructed in the shape of a ring, and when it was covered with white icing it looked like a huge Polo mint.

Sunday 9 December. We have been given some strawberry plants which I set out in the garden alongside the pampas grass. Not the best time to plant, but they may survive.

I felt like cooking a quick curry for our evening meal, and made a lamb *sag* using some of the spinach which was still thriving in the garden. The leaves were perfect for this dish – tender and sweet with juicy stalks. I always fear that I might lose the knack of cooking good curries, especially if I do not make them regularly, but the lamb *sag* was excellent and restored my confidence.

In the evening Rose and I browsed through seed catalogues and started to plan the year's vegetables.

Wednesday 12 December. I have discovered that rowan jelly goes splendidly with fried pig's liver. The sharp and slightly bitter flavour of the jelly blends with the creamy texture and strong taste of the meat.

Thursday 13 December. Our fire smells of onions and sprout peelings; in these uncomfortable days we have begun to bank it up with all the vegetable rubbish we can find, and to use it for cooking as well as heating. An aged black kettle, brewing away at the edge of the flames, provides us with hot water, and there is room on the grate for two saucepans.

Although the weather is bleak and the signs are now clear that we are moving towards a time of economic crisis, the prospect does not depress us. The situation has provided a challenge to our skill and ingenuity; it has forced us to think before we act, and this applies to everything from switching on a light to adapting our cooking habits so that as much food is cooked in one pot as possible to save on fuel. I am confident that we will survive the winter.

Friday 14 December. At the moment there are few vegetables except cabbages, carrots, swedes and parsnips, but Rose did manage to find some golfball-sized turnips, the first of the season.

I thought it would be interesting to cook a 'white meal' using some of the turnips and a large plaice that Rose had bought. I filleted the fish with as much skill as I could muster, given the poor condition of our knives, and then steamed it in milk. With the fish and boiled turnips I served creamed potatoes and a little caper sauce to brighten up the plaice (I always find it rather a dull fish) and also to break up the even whiteness of the rest of the food.

As I cooked, the snow began to fall outside, so it was a meal to match the weather.

Sunday 16 December. In the evening Rose and I had a rare evening out together; we drove to Framlingham, met her parents and her cousin Naomi, and went to the carol service. It was a night for song. The cold cloisters of the church were filled with choirboys in blue and white cassocks, but these boys displayed dirty black shoes and grey socks beneath their religious garb. The whole occasion reminded me of my days as a school choirboy, with a pure treble voice but less than perfect manners.

Throughout the service I was distracted by the thought of the mulled wine that was promised for later in the evening. So when the carolling had ended we went out into the biting air and up the winding back streets of the town to Naomi's house. We arrived to find mulled wine, cheeses and a blazing wood fire, and quickly settled in. The wine was hot and scented with cloves, and it demanded special treatment: it had to be drunk quickly before it got cold and then the glass refilled as soon as possible.

Monday 17 December. Made some vanilla-scented chestnut preserve to take up to Blakeney for Christmas. Hope to use this with the cold turkey on Boxing Day.

Wednesday 19 December. Rose tried to make brandy snaps. She had great difficulty in getting the mixture to the right consistency for twirling. But eventually she mastered the technique and produced a heap of golden coils, crisp and brittle. These were intended as Christmas presents, but the pile soon diminished as we sampled more and more of them.

Early in the evening there was a sound of cautious carol-singers at the door. A large gathering of schoolchildren accompanied on the violin and accordion by supervising adults. We watched as they sang for us.

Sunday 23 December. Final preparations before our Christmas trip to Blakeney. I had planned to make a pâté, but needed some sherry to put in it. So I made an urgent phone call to Rosemary and John to ask if they had any that I could use. John sent over half a bottle.

Spent most of the morning preparing the pâté; I estimated that it cost about 30p without the sherry. Before putting it in the oven I decorated it with sliced oranges and bay leaves. It turned out well, and the strong smell of liver and garlic lingered in the house all day. Rose made some more ginger fudge, also chocolate truffles and dry oatcakes – a special present for Mac.

We received some good food presents during the day: home-made sweets from Trishi, a bottle of tomato ketchup from Elizabeth, and we found a piece of Stilton and a bottle of red wine stuffed into an old coke hod outside our door. We later discovered that these were from the people at the Harbour Inn.

By the evening both Rose and I were exhausted, and sat down to drink a glass of John's sherry.

Monday 24 December. Rose and I set out for Blakeney after lunch with a car loaded up with presents and special foods for Christmas.

After a very large supper of cold pheasant we spent a lazy evening indoors with occasional glasses of malt whisky.

Tuesday 25 December. I had promised to help Rose and Mac with the ponies, so I got up quite early. A very cold morning, but

bright. I started the day with a bowl of porridge dowsed with whisky and milk. This definitely fortified me for my duties.

It was turning into a good day by the time we got back to the cottage, where Barbara was busy basting another huge turkey; it would only fit into the oven with very careful manipulation. Lunch was the predictable but excellent combination of turkey, bacon, stuffing (made by me), roast potatoes, sprouts, sausages, and so on. After we had struggled through this we dealt out presents to one another. For Hannah, going through her first Christmas, this was the best part of the day, although she often thought that the wrappings were more interesting than the presents themselves. She got more and more excited throughout the afternoon and we had a great problem trying to get her to bed. But she had enjoyed her day.

In the evening we tried the pâté that I had made – it was coarse and very rich; and we passed round pieces of Rose's ginger fudge and chocolate truffles.

Friday 28 December. An eventful day. Invited to Rosemary's for a cold lunch; it was a pleasant change to dress up and go out to eat in the middle of the day. Rosemary had worked hard for there was a row of dishes that stretched almost from one end of her long kitchen to the other. I walked the line, sniffing and examining the fare: a banquet-sized plate heaped up with cold turkey; a pâté hidden beneath a layer of pure white pork fat; a pizza like a red wheel, with anchovy spokes and studs of green olives; an immense bowl of cole slaw fortunately not smothered with dressing; creamed artichoke hearts and an onion tart. On the table there were more delights – pickled onions, apricot and orange chutney, apple chutney and a rare Mauritian pickle that they had bought in London. This was syrupy sweet and tasted of ginger.

Eventually we settled down to work our way through the dishes. Hannah, who was with us, caused chaos throughout the meal, sticking her fingers into oranges and ripping the paper tablecloth that had been put down to contain her mischievous games.

We passed away the afternoon with coffee, orange liqueurs and cheroots. As we had eaten so much lunch we felt we could do without supper, and in the evening we went to see a pantomime performed by the local theatre centre. It was a very funny show called *The Plotters of Cabbage Patch Corner*, and it had some excellent characterizations: ants made up to look like American baseball players; 'the red admiral' – a nautical gent in white trousers and bright red blazer which he opened to reveal beautiful gossamer-like patterns on the lining; a spider with dead-white face and dressed in a black morning suit like some figure from Berlin in the 1930s.

A cheerful evening. Finally we visited Rob and had some Scotch and cigars. He gave us a pheasant which we stowed in the back of the car.

Saturday 29 December. Rose brought back sprats from the Harbour. I fried some for lunch and made a kind of *escabeche* with the rest. After frying them I marinaded them in a mixture of oil and vinegar with strips of carrot, chopped onion and bay leaves. I let the dish cool for several hours, and then tried some as a late snack. Left the remainder overnight.

Sunday 30 December. *Escabeche* much improved today. The marinade has had time to affect the flavour and texture of the fish.

In the afternoon Rose and I dealt with the pheasant we had been given. Usually Rose does the plucking and I perform the drawing and trussing, but we thought that the easiest method would be to hold the bird over our dustbin while we stripped the feathers together. Rose much speedier and more expert at the job than I was. Then I took the pheasant into the kitchen where I did the necessary surgery; this is not a task I particularly enjoy although I can manage to do it without much trouble. It is the smell of a high bird that I find most offensive rather than the actual process of scooping out the entrails. Finally I trussed the bird, smothered it with protective pieces of fat bacon and put it in the oven to roast.

Monday 31 December. A damp afternoon, with fog swirling across the fields. It looked as if we would be spending New Year's Eve at home alone, until we remembered the Stilton and red wine we had been given for Christmas, and decided to invite friends over for the evening. I was much cheered by the thought of company.

Had to go through the house to find what we could offer in the way of food; out with the Stilton, a jar of pickled cucumbers, some bread, also gingerbread and Christmas cake. Rose had the idea of mulling the wine, but as the solitary bottle would not last long, she went across the road to the pub, to get extra supplies. First we stuck an orange with cloves and boiled this in water with cinnamon, using the heat of the fire. After this had simmered we tipped in the wine and some sugar and kept the whole lot warm on the grate.

By this time the fog had settled and outside it was bleak and eerie – a lone street lamp lit the scene with an orange glow. Rosemary and John arrived after taking a wrong turning along the road, even though it is little more than a mile of familiar lanes from their house to ours. They needed warming. Before serving them some wine I ceremonially tipped a miniature bottle of brandy into the brew.

Gordon and Elizabeth arrived later with a contribution of wine. I kept the mulling going throughout the evening, mixing, tasting and brewing. We soon needed more wine and had to pay more visits to the pub. The place was deserted except for a quartet of old ladies up at the bar, eating Christmas cake out of a tin, and a man in the corner playing the electric organ.

We waited up for the New Year, saw it through and reluctantly ended our celebrations when the wine ran out.

Tuesday 1 January 1974. Rose made her famous vegetable soup of carrots, parsnips, onions and potatoes. In the evening we had to feed her parents who were visiting for the day and delivering a massive antique wireless; its size and shape seemed to invite watching as well as listening.

We gave them boiled mutton, caper sauce, carrots and parsnips. The quantity of root vegetables – particularly those windy parsnips – consumed during the day made me feel fouly bloated throughout the evening; they wreaked explosive havoc.

Heard that Rosemary and John lost their way again, going home last night. No doubt the combined effect of fog and mulled wine.

Wednesday 2 January. The parsnips continue. Rose made an excellent parsnips *au gratin*, eaten with fried vegetables left over from yesterday. I felt turbulent again afterwards.

Saturday 12 January. We were given three pigeons. I didn't bother to pluck them fully, but only removed the downy breast feathers; these floated around the kitchen and seemed particularly attracted to my nose. I sliced off the breast meat intact and cut it into pieces; the dark colour and sickly sweet smell reminded me of raw pig's kidney.

Rose made a pie with it. I cooked the meat first by frying it lightly in a little mutton dripping; Rose prepared onions and mushrooms and then threw a pastry cover over the mixture. It was a splendid pie. The meat was like the best and most tender steak with a subtle gamey flavour. But I resisted the temptation to finish it off at one sitting, thinking it more sensible to save some for another treat tomorrow.

Tuesday 15 January. Came back from work in the afternoon to find Rose out, and an unrecognizable mixture on the stove. After I had sampled it, I realized it must be celery and apple soup. She had got the idea from a pear chutney that we make which also includes celery; the combination of celery with apple worked equally well. I heated up the soup on the fire and gulped down the whole lot before Rose arrived home.

Wednesday 16 January. The crisis continues to worsen and at the moment we are relying heavily on our fire for heating and cooking to save electricity.

In the afternoon I found a saucepan, apparently full of cabbage, boiling away on the grate, and I asked Rose where the rest of our meal was; I assumed this was simply a pan of vegetables. Rose replied, as if it was obvious, that it was 'under the cabbage'.

The whole meal was contained in one pot like the old 'bargee's pail'. I examined the contents of the saucepan more closely and found that the crisp, white cabbage hid a mixture of bacon, haricot beans and tomatoes. The cabbage was cooking in steam and kept its crispness, although it gradually turned pink, coloured by the juice from the tomatoes.

After supper Rose went off to the local cash-and-carry to buy bulk supplies for the coming months: vinegar, sugar, rice, treacle etc. The price of rice and pulses has soared over the past few weeks, and lentils are now 23p a pound. So even our frugal stand-bys are no longer cheap.

I have seen newspaper reports of lentil-hoarding in Glasgow warehouses.

Saturday 19 January. A pleasant Saturday at home. Rose baked bread and cakes, and covered the kitchen in a fine layer of flour and currants; a warm, yeasty smell in the air. She doesn't do as much baking as she would like to, so these sessions are important. When the oven is in use, she fills it with as many things as possible and spends hours checking temperatures and cooking times, since a fair amount of organization is needed to ensure that all the different cakes and loaves are properly cooked. This approach is very like a baking day in the old style, and it is a useful fuel-saving measure. Today's efforts produced two flat wholemeal loaves, gingerbread, a fruit cake made without eggs and a delicious apple cake.

Hannah was fascinated by the bread. She managed to hold a loaf in both hands and take a large bite out of it while it was still warm.

Sunday 20 January. Rose's parents, her brother Ian and his family down for the day. We had cold turkey and vegetables for lunch which they had brought with them to save us the cooking. Hannah and Sarah (Rose's niece) both gnawed the remains of turkey drumsticks like seasoned gourmets; they cleaned off every scrap of flesh and tossed the bones onto the floor.

To follow the turkey Rose made a treacle pudding, golden and light as a sponge cake. This pleased Mac as he seldom eats such puddings at home. He ate several portions avidly, as if the whole meal had been only a prelude to this rare treat.

With a gallon can of syrup in the house we tend to be rather extravagant, but this will have to stop if we are to keep our economy within reasonable limits.

Tuesday 22 January. Rose and Hannah off to Kent to stay with some friends for a couple of days. Left to fend for myself. As I was rather busy I searched the larder for an easy supper, and found one of my Christmas presents – a tin of squid in its own ink. This would do, eaten with some rice.

The pieces of squid were like tiny mutant hands with fringed fingers. It was a strange, and slightly unnerving experience, as if I was eating the remains of some bizarre criminal episode. But I recognized the taste and texture immediately, and thought again of my Spanish holiday with its *calamares Romanos* (rings of large squid cooked in batter), and *pulpito* (small octopus fried whole), which I had first discovered in a dingy bar with a sawdust floor, hidden away in the back streets of Barcelona. Here I would eat fried chicken necks, whole sheep's jawbones with the tongues dangling from them, and aubergines – again sliced and deep-fried.

And I would drink quantities of milky *horchata* and cheap cognac as I watched scraggy dogs devouring the scraps that were thrown to them by customers.

Wednesday 23 January. Travelled down to London on the coach. The weather in Blythburgh when I started out was dry and very windy, but London and later Berkhamsted offered only the dismal sight of steady rain, hour after hour; we seldom see these conditions in our part of East Anglia.

It was good to see my family and old friends again. Richard, Alan and Alastair were all in various states of depression, but not so involved with their financial, emotional and professional difficulties that they could refuse a drink with me. Good beer in the Swan.

Thursday 24 January. Up to London for the day. Before getting the train I met Alastair in the Swan for an early pint at 10.30. We were lone beer-drinkers among old ladies with shopping bags and sensible cups of coffee.

Met Richard S. and presented him with some fudge that Rose had made. He was pleased. We had lunch in a small Italian restaurant in Covent Garden; I began with spare ribs fried with garlic and rosemary which were very good – dry but moistened by their own fat. Then *medaglioni alla marina* – pork fillet covered with a cheese sauce in which there were chopped tomatoes, prawns and mussels. This was marred by the fact that the mussels were obviously not fresh, but had that characteristic vinegar flavour – a sure sign that they had come from a bottle. There is no excuse for this, especially in the middle of the mussel season. Still it was enough for me to have a leisurely lunch and copious quantities of red wine all provided, and in any case I was in no mood for complaining.

Back to Berkhamsted in the evening. After a long session in the Swan, we visited the Chinese take-away, and my brother treated us to barbecued spare-ribs. These were very different to the ones I had earlier in the day – they were moist, scented and aromatic, and were almost completely lean. The choice was a wise, functional one, since the ribs could be eaten like chips, straight from their hot foil containers. I burnt my fingers delving too eagerly, and had to protect myself with a handkerchief. We giggled drunkenly as we dipped the ribs into their rich sauce, and loitered outside the restaurant long after we had finished eating.

A memorable day's food.

Friday 25 January. To London again for another lunch; this time to posh but cosmopolitan Bertorelli's. First smoked turkey – a little dry and served as slices from a boned rolled sausage. Then red mullet *meunière* with spinach and new potatoes. Finished with Stilton, coffee and brandy. Did not leave the restaurant till nearly 4 in the afternoon.

Back to Suffolk by the coach. In Blythburgh before closing time, so I had a quick pint to restore myself after the tedious journey.

Tuesday 29 January. We are in the season of Seville oranges. Although Rose and I had searched markets and shops, we had been unable to find any cheaper than 11p a pound. This is a dramatic rise since last year, and it doesn't look as if they will get any cheaper, so we decided to buy some of this quite expensive fruit for marmalade.

Rose is the marmalade expert, but this time I helped her with some of the preparation. We chopped orange and lemon peel round the warmth of our fire until our hands stung with the juice. She was making a dark, coarse-cut marmalade which included spoonfuls of treacle. The cooking went well, although we had to use the stove instead of the fire, and after I had helped with the potting I scraped the remains of the warm, half-set marmalade from the sides of the preserving pan, to taste what we had made.

Wednesday 30 January. My birthday. I have reached twenty-seven years of age. For breakfast I tried the marmalade: very rich, but the peel a little chewy. It will mellow with age, for this type of preserve is best when it is ancient and syrupy.

Otherwise an indifferent, uneventful day.

Sunday 3 February. Boiled some pieces of belly pork for supper. John, after a day's shooting, gave us two drawn and plucked pigeons.

Monday 4 February. Tough weather with dangerous gales. In many parts of the country there have been floods, and trees down, but here it is simply blowing hard, which makes my journeys on the bicycle agonizing, exhausting work.

For supper a warming pigeon stew with rich stock from yesterday's pork, deliciously flavoured with celery. Because the birds were recently killed, they had not acquired a gamey flavour, but were still moist and tender. It was difficult and frustrating trying to manipulate a knife and fork to get the meat from the frail carcases, so Rose and I soon discarded these tools and used our fingers.

Enough stock left over for tomorrow's cottage pie.

Wednesday 6 February. Richard arrived for a few days. A turn in the weather; as well as gales there is now torrential rain, not the usual brief showers that we expect in this part of the country, but a steady, unrelenting downpour.

For supper a cross between a *cassoulet* and the old Boston baked beans – haricot beans cooked with onions, tomatoes and black treacle. Into this mixture we put chopped bacon pieces from a hock and slices of smoked boiling sausage, and left the saucepan to simmer by the fire all afternoon.

Rose started to prepare some grapefruit and lemon marmalade, but soon had to abandon the operation. Apparently the old tights she was using instead of muslin to hold the pips had leaked dye into the marmalade and it was ruined. She put the saucepan and its contents outside and let it fill up with rain.

Decided to spend the weekend in Blakeney and to take Richard with us; it will be an opportunity for him to see old friends.

Thursday 7 February. In the evening Richard and I decided to visit the Badingham White Horse. We had passed this pub many times before and always thought that it looked promising, so tonight we set out to see what it was like. We were expecting to have a couple of quiet drinks and then come home.

A small untidy public bar, but with an extraordinary

atmosphere. It was crowded out, and everyone was singing. The leader was a huge toothless man called Jim with a glass in one hand and a bottle of light ale in the other. He was waving his arms madly as he sang. They were obviously not used to strangers, but the drinking and singing continued regardless of us. In one corner an old man nodded his head in approval.

It wasn't long before we were bought a drink and after that we were hard pressed to keep up with the regulars. It was clear why most of them were drinking from half-pint mugs; the speed of the rounds would make drinking pints quite impossible. We listened, smiled and cheered Jim as he finished each song, and by the time we left the pub we were astonishingly drunk.

Friday 8 February. To Blakeney in the afternoon. The weather appalling, cold and rainy; we were grateful for the comfort and speed of Richard's car.

For supper a large piece of belly of pork roasted; it had crisp golden crackling. Barbara had cooked some cabbage with fennel seeds, and Richard particularly appreciated this. We drank from a large bottle of red wine.

Did not go out in the evening.

Saturday 9 February. As we did not have anything to drink yesterday evening, Richard and I were eager to go to the pub at lunchtime. The White Horse, where we used to enjoy ourselves, has changed hands; it now smells of new paint and perfume, and the whole place glistens with fruit machines. So we now drink in one of the quayside hotels – not ideal, but at least they do sell Adnams bitter.

A long session, and we did not leave till closing-time. Then back to the house to have sausage sandwiches, spread thickly with mustard, and some whisky. Richard and I made an unsteady journey through the village to see Mike and Pooh. As usual hordes of children in their house, and we found Pooh casually gutting pheasants; a foul smell in the kitchen. I think we were embarrassingly drunk, but it was good to see them again, and they were pleased to see us and quite tolerant of our behaviour.

For supper a piece of fatty brisket and more red wine, then to the pub again late in the evening. Everyone sitting around the bar and time passing very slowly. It was like being encapsulated, suspended inside the small circular room; no one coming or going. We sat, drank and waited for closing-time to break the spell.

I felt dizzy and unwell when we got home, and had to take a walk down to the quay.

Sunday 10 February. Richard moved off to stay with other friends in the area. Rose and I returned to Suffolk after lunch; no change in the dismal weather.

Sunday 17 February. Rose, Hannah and I went out together for a walk. A hopeful spring morning. We walked round 'the gluepot' – a pleasant route that circuits our village, but I have no idea why it was given that name. The roadsides speckled with the bright blue of flowering speedwells; green luxuriant alexanders everywhere.

When we got back, Gordon and Elizabeth invited us over for lunch: pieces of chicken casseroled with tarragon. We supplied a bottle of wine to go with the meal.

Monday 25 February. Saw a barn owl perching in a dead tree alongside the A12. It seemed to be scrutinizing the traffic. I suspect it was the same bird that I saw in the same spot almost exactly a year ago.

Friday 1 March. Invited to Rosemary's for supper. A bitterly cold night, but I was in good spirits and determined to enjoy myself. The meal began with an impressive kipper mousse, moulded in the shape of a fish and jokingly decorated with a pair of currants for eyes. The mousse was surrounded by chunks of lemon and cucumber, and it was creamy and seemed to evaporate in the mouth. Rosemary followed this with a much more substantial dish of stuffed chicken breasts with mushrooms; she felt that this had been left too long in the oven, but apart from a certain dryness in the mushrooms themselves it was excellent. By the time we had finished this huge course we should have been full, but Rosemary then offered us an apricotina which it was impossible to refuse.

It was a light-hearted, friendly gathering that ended with belly-laughs as we listened to old records of Tom Lehrer.

Wednesday 6 March. Rose to Blakeney for a few days to do some work with the ponies. I got a lift to Norwich with John, and was invited back for supper; Rosemary had cooked a special Indian meal for me. But as soon as I ventured into the kitchen she collared me and insisted that I deal with cooking the pappadoms. I think I have finally found the best way to cook these after years of trying. The secret is to use quite a lot of oil and literally immerse the pappadom; it should not need turning and after a few seconds it should have expanded, changed colour and become crisp. In the past I tended to use too little oil with the result that the pappadoms often burned and puffed up unevenly into odd shapes.

Rosemary had cooked a beef and tomato curry, rather like a *rogan ghosht* but more liquid. With the pappadoms, some perfect boiled rice, chutneys and yoghurt, it was a real feast, and I was impressed with Rosemary's skill as a cook of Indian food.

Friday 8 March. Took a bottle of red wine and some cigars over to Rosemary and John's house in the evening. A clear night and pleasantly cool. It was a joy to ride along the lanes in the dark; the air seemed clean and exhilarating like early morning at the seaside.

In return for the wine, they produced some smoked sprats; these were small but as sweet as any I have tasted.

Sunday 10 March. Rose brought back a piece of pork from Blakeney, and I prepared this for roasting. I took great care to get the crackling as crisp as possible by rubbing it with salt and oil, and by carefully adjusting the oven temperature during cooking. It turned out well.

As a change from apple sauce, I had the idea of making a rich apricot sauce along the same lines, using dried apricots, butter, brown sugar and a pinch of nutmeg.

Saturday 16 March. Organized a day trip to London to hear a performance of Gordon's new opera; went with Felicity, Rob, Rosemary and John, and travelled down in a vast estate car like a coach with three rows of seats. Stopped at a roadside pub near

Ilford to have some lunch and to break up the journey. A most gloomy and unfriendly place, formica everywhere. The barman was rude to us, the food was dreadful and we got out as quickly as possible. It was to be the first of many harassments during the day.

Once in London we searched for somewhere to have a snack before the performance. Rosemary and John knew a cheap Greek café in the West End, but Rob was rather shocked by the simplicity of the place, open to the road, with no kitchen – only grills, hot-plates and turning spits near the entrance. But we had a good meal: Greek bread shaped like a pocket and stuffed with grilled paper-thin slices of lamb and vegetables. I think that Rob was pleasantly surprised. But I was accosted by one of the waiters on the way out and accused of not paying the bill. The others had gone ahead of me, and I was temporarily stranded, trying to explain that they had paid for everything. Fortunately the situation was sorted out without any trouble.

We made our way towards the Coliseum and quite by chance ran into Gordon. He took us for a cup of tea in a nearby café. We waited to be served, but were quickly evicted; apparently we could not have tea unless we had food as well. By now the signs were definitely against us, and we headed for the nearest pub to calm ourselves ready for the evening. We presented Gordon with a bottle of Glenmorangie – his favourite whisky – and discussed where we would eat after the opera. I wanted an Indian meal but Rob wasn't used to the food, so we tactfully decided on another East European meal at a slightly smarter kebab house, and arranged to meet Gordon there.

The opera itself was magnificent and it affected Rose to such an extent that she rushed up to Gordon afterwards and kissed him.

But our troubles were not over. I was confident that I knew the way to the restaurant, but was soon well off course, deceived by the changed appearance of London streets at night. But we found the place, it was still open, and Gordon was patiently waiting for us. We gorged ourselves on *hummus*, *tahina* (sesame-seed paste), kebabs and *sheftalia* and drank much red wine. We lingered over cups of Turkish coffee and plates of perfumed Turkish delight provided free by friendly waiters. A satisfying and trouble-free end to our day.

The journey home was long and tedious.

Tuesday 19 March. Rose busy making cakes and jellies for Hannah's birthday party tomorrow.

Wednesday 20 March. Hannah's birthday. In the afternoon lots of her friends – all older than herself – arrived for the party. Typically she was the centre of attention and picked at every sort of food. It was a happy, if slightly chaotic affair.

Thursday 21 March. Blackthorn flowers stranded like snowflakes in the hedges. Lambs playing in the fields. Rooks building in the trees near our cottage.

Saturday 23 March. Rob held a party; lots of drink and the promise of some good food. Rosemary arrived looking as if she had just spent a month in the Caribbean; her face shone like a bronze sculpture. A great party. I was very merry and danced for the first time in years. I could still perform quite well, although I swayed and spun rather unsteadily.

Then it was time for food; an extraordinary display. There was lemon chicken, a kind of Mexican rice with peppers, mushrooms and chicken (the rice itself rather stodgy), and a whole row of rich desserts, puddings and flans. As the old rock records played I talked with Rosemary until everyone had vanished from the food room. I gnawed at chicken wings and tried to restore her self-confidence; she was greatly oppressed. Then back to the party, more dancing and drink. I mentioned the idea of a curry evening in which we could share the cooking; it would be an opportunity to introduce Rob to Indian food.

The party dragged on into the early hours, but we were all tired out, so we drifted home.

Sunday 31 March. Rose went to a horse show in Ipswich, and I decided to stay at home as I had a rough cold. But the morning was bright and warm, so I cycled over to see Rosemary and John, and was invited to lunch.

John suggested a barbecue, but first we had to go down the road to pick up the apparatus, which he had lent to a friend. We carried it back on a wheelbarrow. After setting up the barbecue we lit the charcoal and got ready to cook pieces of pork and chicken, which I had carved and jointed. The charcoal took a long while to heat up, so we drank some cool white wine while we were waiting. At last the charcoal was hot and white and we laid the pieces of meat on the grid to cook; we really should have cleaned this first because it produced rusty imprints on the meat, still we managed to scrape these off.

The morning was hot like summer and it was a slow but enjoyable task tending the food in the sun. But Rosemary's children became very impatient. The results of our efforts were quite good, not as impressive as I had anticipated, but the chicken in particular did have a special flavour.

Wednesday 3 April. Rose did a large baking session and produced some memorable round pasties made from mince, potato, onion and herbs.

Friday 5 April. Visited the Indian spice shop in Norwich to get the first load of supplies for the curry evening later this month. The shop sells an amazing selection of spices, herbs, pulses, rice, pickles, flour, and mostly quite cheap. (I bought paprika for 2p an ounce.) I had hoped to get some Indian vegetables as well, but they had none in stock, so as well as spices I bought lime pickle, pappadoms, and *besan* (chick-pea) flour.

Monday 8 April. Along the hedgerows the alexanders are thrusting buds like fists.

Friday 12 April. Bright spring weather. We have been busy digging up part of our lawn to make vegetable beds, and today Rose planted seeds: leeks, shallots, radishes, beetroot, broad beans. The strawberries which I put in during the winter have survived and are beginning to show new leaves; I hope they will fruit later in the year.

Monday 15 April. Went over to Rosemary's with Indian cook books to discuss Saturday's meal. It was a chill evening, but the ride along almost dark lanes was exciting.

Rosemary and I had agreed to share the cooking; she was going to make another of her meat and tomato curries, a cucumber *raitha*, rice and chappatis. I was planning a *dhal*, also a small dish of prawns marinaded and grilled, and I was debating whether to attempt a kind of *tandoori* chicken. Originally I had the idea of dividing the meal into courses – not the Indian way, but it might simplify the serving of the meal.

During the evening we modified many of these plans. I was very dubious about the *tandoori*, and we both agreed that it would probably be as easy to serve all the dishes together if we designed the menu sensibly. So I abandoned my original scheme and thought again. Eventually we drew up a balanced menu: the beef and tomato curry and a kind of *murgh massalam* would be the centrepieces of the meal, and they would be flanked by one dish of boiled rice and another of pilau rice with prawns. There would also be a *dhal*, vegetable curries and a tray of side dishes – pappadoms, *raitha*, Bombay ducks, chappatis, chutneys and pickles.

We agreed to hold the party at Rosemary's house since there is more room there than in our cottage. After the meal we would need the space of her long sitting-room to relax in.

Thursday 18 April. To Norwich to get the rest of the ingredients for the meal. Mainly vegetables – very expensive *bhindis*, green chillies, garlic and spring onions. Also more spices, split peas, yoghurt, etc.

Friday 19 April. In the morning I began preparations for the curries. First job, before I went out gardening, was to skin and joint a chicken and spread it with yoghurt, coriander and finely chopped green chillies. I left this to marinade all day. Also put the split peas to soak.

After supper I got to work on the *murgh massalam*. The plan was to set the pieces of spiced chicken on a bed of spring onions, but after completing the dish I wasn't satisfied; the chicken itself was perfect, but the spring onions had absorbed so much oil and butter that they were virtually inedible. I rescued the chicken and threw out the onions.

By the end of the evening I also had the *dhal* ready. It was bright yellow and sharp with the taste of lemon juice.

Saturday 20 April. Worked all afternoon on my special dishes. The chicken from the *murgh massalam* was rather a problem, but I managed to make use of it by surrounding it with fried *bhindis*. I had to fry Bombay ducks, so I opened all the windows, well aware of the stench that these can make when they are being cooked. I parboiled some saffron rice and collected together the shelled prawns, blanched almonds, tomatoes and grated coconut that would make up the dish. I put these into little plastic bags because later we would have to transport everything to Rosemary's. When I had finished cooking I took a rest and biked over to Wenhaston to see how Rosemary was getting on.

She had made two large dishes of her beef and tomato curry, and wisely kept one of them mild. The other was hot and I could see the dried chillies floating among pieces of beef. Her *raitha* was cooling in the fridge and John was having fun with a vegetable curry. So far no problems.

I went home to get changed, organize myself and wait for John to pick me up. Rose arrived back from a horse show and leapt into the bath. When John arrived we loaded up the car, carefully balancing the dishes so that they did not spill their contents over the seats. I almost forgot the vital chives – for the *dhal* – but picked some before we set out.

Once settled in Rosemary's kitchen, John and I failed after many attempts to make successful chappatis, and we juggled with dishes in the oven. The meal was almost ready and we had only to lay out the food on the table, an important step. We closed the doors of the dining-room when our friends arrived, and then, at just the right moment, we led them in to eat. It was a startling display, arranged just as we had planned it. After briefly explaining the various dishes, I left each person to fend for himself. Rob took his first cautious mouthful, and he was slowly converted to the food. The meal was going well until Rose bit on a chilli; she went bright red and gasped, but it was soon over. Others chewed cardamom seeds without twitching. My only disappointment was that the *bhindis* and rice were not as good as they should have been; they had not stood up well to the transportation and the re-heating.

The whole meal must have taken an hour to eat, and we ate until we could eat no more. For Rosemary and myself it was a satisfying and triumphant moment. As we recovered I sat in a corner of the sitting-room and played records for the others.

Sunday 21 April. I had volunteered to help Rosemary with the daunting amount of washing-up left after the meal, and I cycled over in the morning. But it was done when I arrived, so we sat and reminisced about the evening before. I stayed for a lunch of remnants – curry, rice, pappadoms, pickles. Rosemary's children were fascinated by the pappadoms as I demonstrated the mysteries of cooking them.

Wednesday 24 April. Now that the weather is good and the evenings are long, Rose is out almost every day riding the ponies. This has caused some disruption of our eating habits. I cook most of the meals, and have to organize the food so that there is something edible for Rose when she gets back.

Although we are still struggling against rising food prices, we are coping more easily now that we need less fuel for heating, and can rely on a supply of fresh garden vegetables.

Saturday 27 April. Rose, cooking a rare meal, produced some fine herrings in oatmeal. She had used precisely the right amount of oats, so that the outside of the fish was crisp and lightly brown, and not saturated with oil. We ate the herrings with bright green sprouting broccoli and mustard sauce. I mashed the soft roe from my fish with the sauce to make a rich paste.

Sunday 28 April. I ate the last of the packet of pappadoms with some leek flan and toad-in-the-hole.

Tuesday 30 April. Heard my first cuckoo far out across the heathland. And tonight we had our first salad of the year – a slab of cold pork pie with tomatoes, spring onions, potato salad and cress.

Thursday 2 May. A pair of swallows diving at sparrows on a newly seeded field. The weather unpredictable, changing from the blackest thunderclouds to a clear summer sky in the space of an hour. We still need a good rain.

Rose planted two tomato plants and some young cabbages along the back of a flower bed. A rabbit has nibbled at our spinach.

Sunday 5 May. Rose had bought a chunky piece of pork loin, very meaty, and I used it to make a variant of *mishmishiya* – a traditional Middle Eastern stew based on mutton and apricots. I chopped the pork into small pieces and let it stew very slowly all afternoon with dried apricots, cinnamon, bay leaves, onion and garlic, with a couple of dried chillies added.

By evening the meat was beautifully tender and the apricots had formed a thick sauce; I served the dish on some rice. It was excellent although the effect of the chillies was too much for Rose; but she struggled bravely on, and by eating a little of the pork slowly with a lot of rice, she eventually finished her portion.

Amazing how strong dried chillies can be if allowed to cook for a long while.

Thursday 8 May. The local toddlers collected at our house for the afternoon.

I got back to find the kitchen smelling of vinegar, and saw the remains of my gallon jar of pickled onions scattered around the room; onions rolling about on the floor. Apparently Hannah and one of her friends had sneaked away from the others to enjoy themselves in the kitchen; Rose found Hannah sitting on the table, and the other child staring at the mess of onions and glass.

Monday 13 May. The White Hart now sells smoked mackerel. These are whole fish, hot-smoked so that they are cooked, and they look extraordinary. They are huge, especially alongside smoked trout, and their skins are golden with an odd corrugated appearance. At first they looked so daunting laid out whole that people did not know what to do with them; so now they are filleted and then put on display.

It is unusual to see this type of smoked mackerel in Suffolk; normally the fish are split and cold-smoked like kippers.

Friday 17 May. The weather is so dry that the young vegetables will not grow. Birds and rabbits are attacking them.

Tuesday 21 May. Gordon made cinnamon toast at teatime for friends and myself. He told us that this was one of his staple foods as a student when he frequented the coffee-houses of Oxford. The toast was delicious, buttered and sprinkled with brown sugar and ground cinnamon, and put under the grill so that the sugar started to melt.

Rose pulled the first of our early radishes.

Wednesday 22 May. It looks as if the weather has turned at last; heavy rain today, but it will need to continue for a week before the ground is cured of the drought.

I felt rather queasy and delicate all day. We had the remains of a roast chicken, and I had planned on making a quick curry, but now I felt my body could not withstand such an onslaught. So I settled for a mild fricassee instead; with its cream, butter and herbs it was a soothing meal.

In the evening Elizabeth rang me up, asking my advice about making a *raitha*; she had mixed the ingredients, but the result was not good. The main point about a *raitha* is that it should be left to cool in the fridge for as long as possible. My recipe includes yoghurt, cream and beaten egg whites, and the texture of this is greatly improved if it is allowed to cool for several hours.

Thursday 23 May. Saw an apple tree with so much blossom that the whole tree appeared white, with hardly a trace of green

leaves. Many ancient apple trees in this area are flowering for the first time in years, and with luck they may fruit in the summer.

Friday 24 May. The rain was short-lived and made little impression on the ground. Today blazing hot and dry again. In our garden the only vegetables that have grown substantially are the broad beans. Everything else – spinach, peas, beetroot and lettuce in particular – is at a standstill regardless of the watering we do.

For supper a salad decorated with fennel. The smell of garlic and vinaigrette lingered in the kitchen all evening.

Sunday 26 May. The flowers of the horse chestnut are standing like fat candles on a Christmas tree.

Rose made a treacle tart perfumed with orange peel.

Monday 3 June. Gooseberries ready for picking. We don't have fruit bushes in our Bramfield garden, except for a patch of thorny gooseberry that forms part of an extraordinary composite hedge along with hawthorn, briar rose, comfrey and young sycamore. Still, in one of the gardens that I look after there are four gigantic gooseberry bushes, laden with fruit. In fact there are two distinct varieties: as well as almost hairless fruit the size of small plums, there are tiny spherical fruits, very whiskery, which are the best for eating fresh when they are very ripe.

One of the advantages of being a gardener is the free access to fruit and vegetables; this produce is really part of my wages. Today I took home several pounds of weighty dessert gooseberries; I had picked them without gloves and my hands were scratched and sore.

Tuesday 4 June. Rose's parents here for the day. Mac and I went to the Bell soon after evening opening-time; no one in the place. I was mistakenly given mild instead of bitter, but I drank it all the same. The first mild I have had since last summer, and it was good; no trace of that sickly sweet taste. It was easy to drink, and I had disposed of three pints within half an hour – those straight glasses make drinking so simple. We were very tempted to stay and talk with the landlord, but eventually emptied our glasses for the last time and ambled back to the house.

The dining table was strewn with an assortment of cold meat and salads for our supper: some tasteless pre-packed salami and garlic sausage, very good Melton Mowbray pork pie, cheeses, tomatoes, potato salad.

Wednesday 5 June. I made a pie with some fresh haddock fillets. I steamed the fish in milk, lifted off the flesh, put this in a dish and covered it with sliced hard-boiled pheasant eggs. (These are plentiful at the moment and are much cheaper than hen eggs.) I poured mustard sauce over the fish and eggs and covered the pie with mashed potato.

At the moment our meals are often undistinguished, and are based more on the functional necessity of eating within the limits of both money and time. Rose is out a great deal, and I tend to continue gardening fairly late, so we have to rely on quick meals that are not spoiled if kept hot for some time.

Friday 7 June. Rose used up some of the gooseberries in a fool.

Monday 11 June. The weather has been hot and dry for weeks, with only the occasional day of rain. The effect of this on the supply of vegetables has been drastic. Everything is late – the first broad beans are just beginning to come on the market – and prices are ludicrously high.

But today we scoured the garden and managed to pick enough spinach for a meal. At least we have one vegetable that we can rely on, provided we can protect the plants from our scavenging rabbit.

Thursday 20 June. Went to Norwich. Searched the market for bargain fruit and vegetables, but could only find some cheap cauliflowers at 5p each. These were small and did not look very appetizing, but the price was reasonable so I bought two. They might be useful for the weekend when Richard is here.

Rose made a cauliflower cheese with one of the misshapen specimens I brought home. The taste was dull and watery.

Friday 21 June. We were given several pounds of young broad beans.

Saturday 22 June. In the morning I picked a large crinkly lettuce and some gooseberries from one of my gardens and went to Southwold to get supplies for the weekend. Richard was due to arrive about teatime and I had planned a light meal of kedgeree and salads before we went out drinking.

I spent the afternoon making the kedgeree and also a tomato salad with thyme, decorated with sprigs of purple-flowered sage, and another salad made from broad beans and chopped fennel. The food appealed to Richard for two reasons: it had the colour and arrangement that he values so highly in Japanese cooking, and it was a step towards the old herbal notion of the salad. He enjoyed the meal greatly.

I persuaded Rose to come to the pub with us, and we arranged to meet Rosemary and John. We had a good deal to drink, Rose went back on the gin, and John enjoyed his first Broadsides. Went to Rosemary's at closing-time, for bulky chicken sandwiches and whisky.

Sunday 23 June. Walked in the afternoon with Richard, and discussed the evening meal. I persuaded him to make some *schwarzwurtz* (comfrey leaves fried in batter), and I was planning some roast belly of pork with apricot sauce and cauliflower, followed by a dish of fresh strawberries that Richard had bought for us.

Rose had problems with the ponies, and as a result our meal plans were disrupted. We decided to postpone the *schwarzwurtz.* When at last we were able to eat, I found that the cauliflower was riddled with maggots – I should have expected this. But the rest of the meal was good, although it was eaten amid chaos with people coming and going. After we had finished eating Trishi appeared with a bottle of home-brewed beer and some powerful punch. We tasted these and suggested that the time was right for Richard to prepare the comfrey. We sat round the table with the greasy leaves and the strong cloudy beer.

Trishi invited us to her party next weekend.

Monday 24 June. Richard went home with a tray of pheasant eggs and a bag of gooseberries.

Wednesday 26 June. We bought the last tray of pheasant eggs from the local shop; there will be no more this season, so I pickled two dozen in vinegar.

Saturday 29 June. Trishi's party. A clear, warm evening – ideal for a big open-air gathering. She had converted two barns into a dance hall and a functional area for food and drink. A couple of hundred people, wandering through the meadows, slumped on hay bales or in tight groups drinking from bottles and paper cups. At first Rose and I felt rather aged among the hoards of fleshy schoolgirls, but soon settled in to drink and dance.

The centrepiece of the drink was Trishi's home-brewed punch which was dispensed from a milk churn with ladles. It was filled out with fresh strawberries and oranges, and was deceptively potent. By midnight, girls were collapsing all around us.

Monday 1 July. Visited the Harbour in the evening with John to discuss playing in the jazz band. John has resurrected his clarinet and I am trying to rediscover my old skills on the guitar. Everything organized for a session next week. The beer slipped down very easily; it was in perfect condition despite the warm weather. This is always critical because the pub has no cellar.

John took home a box of freshly caught plaice and soles, and he was kind enough to offer me some. Food for tomorrow.

Tuesday 2 July. For breakfast I fried one of the plaice that John had given me. Almost for the first time the fish had a good flavour; not at all the dull, watery taste that I have learned to expect. The flesh was firm and white, and had the sweetness of prime whiting.

Rose and I shared a sole and another plaice for our supper. Skinning the sole was a long, awkward business; I am always too cautious with tasks like this.

Thursday 4 July. After a bright morning the weather broke, and it rained heavily for most of the afternoon. I was doing some gardening at Gordon's where he told me about a lute recital at Blythburgh church in the evening, which was to be followed by a meal at his house. I knew nothing of this. Had to make hasty arrangements about transport etc. as Rose felt rather tired and decided not to come out.

The concert was a delightful mixture of songs and instrumental pieces although the setting didn't really match the intimacy of the music. I learned that the meal was to be on a fairly grand scale – the usual friends plus a couple whom I did not know. Each family was contributing one special dish to the meal. Rosemary produced the first course – cold salmon trout with rich Hellman's mayonnaise. Then Elizabeth offered a *navarin* of lamb with young vegetables, and finally Felicity with her usual expertise dished up her desserts, a pavlova and a multi-coloured fruit tart designed in strips. By this time we were all full, but managed to eat some weightless cheesecake and work our way through several bottles of wine.

Friday 5 July. Feeling exhausted; the cumulative effect of many late nights.

Sunday 7 July. We had been given another load of gooseberries, so Rose decided it was time to make some jams and jellies. She put aside the best and largest fruit for jam, and used the rest for jelly. I suggested flavouring this with elderflowers and was lucky to pick some that were still in good condition.

Rose used the rest of the fruit to make some gooseberry and orange jam. This is a combination we have tried before in other dishes such as crumbles and tarts, and it makes a most interesting jam; the orange juice adds just the right amount of sharpness to the soft gooseberries.

Wednesday 10 July. John and I went down to the Harbour for our first session in the band; both of us nervous so we arrived early to have a few drinks before we started. The band performs in the dingy lower bar of the pub, clustered around an unplayable piano. I seated myself alongside the banjo player, and John joined the front line; we were ready to begin. It was a marvellous feeling to be playing in a band again; I got used to the ragged starts and uncertain endings, and it was exciting to be part of the driving rhythm section; I was soon sweating.

The evening went well, and John and I were invited to play again.

Saturday 13 July. Picked the first of our broad beans. It promises to be a good crop, many pods are forming, and there is no sign of black fly as yet. Ate the beans with some slices of fried belly of pork.

Wednesday 17 July. The weather still very dry, but not particularly warm. Peas almost ready for picking; onions and shallots beginning to swell.

I tried the first of my pickled pheasants' eggs. These did not quite match up to hens' eggs as a pickle; the white tended to be rather soft, without that characteristic solid rubbery texture. And the yolk lacked the same creamy flavour.

Friday 19 July. A dry sunny morning, so I took the opportunity of collecting a bag of champignons from the fairy rings that have sprung up on one of my lawns. It would be a great waste to sacrifice them all to the mower, particularly as they are almost the only edible fungus available at the moment.

After supper I set to work to dry the champignons. I put them on trays in the oven until they were crisp. While they were drying I prepared some raspberry vinegar using a couple of pounds of fruit that we had been given. I had already steeped the raspberries in vinegar for two days, and all I now had to do was to strain off the clear red liquid and boil it up with sugar. The vinegar changed colour quite noticeably from bright red to crimson as it was heated, but it remained perfectly clear.

Sunday 21 July. Picked the first peas. Not a great number, but enough for Rose and myself; Hannah stole and sucked the empty pods. We ate the peas with a slab of hake – a fish that is often underrated and put in the same category as plaice.

Wednesday 24 July. Cooked some mince and potatoes for a shepherd's pie, a meal we often eat when we are short of time and money.

Friday 2 August. Rose off to a horse show near Blakeney for a couple of days. For supper I made things easy for myself; I picked a load of our broad beans which are now thriving with large full pods, and I cooked and ate them with a smoked boiling sausage.

I saved some of the broad beans and half the sausage for my lunch tomorrow.

Saturday 3 August. A glorious sunny day. I ate up the remains of the beans and sausage and shared the food with Hannah. Decided to have a light economy meal for my supper – a mushroom omelette with some fresh spinach from the garden.

Sunday 4 August. We are still in a very dry spell, with long days of hot weather and no sign of rain. I took the opportunity of doing some work in our garden, which has been neglected lately. First job was to lift my onions which were fully grown and had drooping yellow tops. Like last year they have done well, in fact I think that they are probably even bigger, with flat firm bulbs. I rubbed all the excess earth from them, and spread them on a large polythene sheet to dry in the sun before hanging them up. I must remember to keep an eye on them in case it rains suddenly.

In the space left by the onions I planted out some of our leeks, which are beginning to grow tall and thin.

Wednesday 6 August. Had to make a rush trip to London; took the offer of an early morning lift with Gordon. I had lunch in an Indian restaurant in Old Brompton Road, which he had recommended to me. I tested the chicken *bhuna* which was very good indeed, and if all the dishes are of the same quality it must surely rate as one of the best in London. It is one of the few restaurants that still provides chutneys free of charge.

After a meeting in the afternoon, I went to stay overnight with some friends. Drank red wine continuously throughout the evening. Paul had to do the cooking, with very little in the house; but he managed to throw together some spaghetti with chopped bacon and herbs.

Back to Suffolk tomorrow.

Saturday 10 August. The dry weather has caused a great growth of flowers in our garden. There are huge teasels, evening primroses and hollyhocks, some eight feet high, all growing fast, fighting for the light. The display is so dense that it almost conceals two sides of the cottage. But the dryness has not been beneficial to our vegetables, although we have peas, broad beans, onions, shallots, radishes and some very healthy beetroot and spinach. Our cauliflowers, after a promising start, are showing signs of bolting.

Wednesday 14 August. We were given a large courgette during the day, which we used to make a *ratatouille* for supper. Invited John to eat with us. I hurried home early from gardening to help Rose with the cooking and house-cleaning before John arrived.

A large meal of pork chops, *ratatouille* and tiny french beans; then John and I left for the Harbour to play another session with the band.

Friday 16 August. To Berkhamsted for the weekend. Had a lively evening in the Swan, drank a good deal of beer and enjoyed myself. Alan in very good form, full of jokes, stories and puns. After closing time we went to the Chinese take-away and bought spare-ribs and pancake rolls, also some fried bean sprouts. We clustered outside on the pavement, around an ancient stone water-trough, and ate the food with our fingers. There is one advantage with the take-away style of eating and that is the freshness of the food; there is a very fast turnover, particularly on Friday evenings, and everything is cooked to order. There is no need for the cooking and reheating of food that is characteristic of so many restaurants. We noticed this with the bean sprouts, which were some of the crispest I have ever eaten; not at all stringy or soggy with oil. The pancake rolls were almost too hot to bite into, and were filled with a mixture of chopped pork, bean sprouts, etc. that had also been freshly cooked. We went home with greasy hands and full stomachs.

Saturday 17 August. Richard took me to one of the recently opened Indian restaurants in Hemel Hempstead. A most interesting meal. I had a superb chicken madras with *bhindi bhaji*; the *bhindis* themselves were small and fat and were not at all mushy – their neat rows of seeds were still intact. From the variety of dishes that we ordered it was clear that this was a restaurant with character; each dish was prepared separately, not from some basic spicy stock. I suspect that this place will become a regular haunt for us in the future.

With my mouth still burning, and my stomach feeling full and hot, I went with Richard and the others to the Crown and Sceptre, where they now sell Young's beer. The second revelation of the day. The bitter, quite as good as Adnams, but with a stronger flavour and more potent. After a slow start – the curry plus four glasses of gassy lager had left me bloated and unable to drink – I gradually recovered and consumed several pints before the evening was over.

Sunday 18 August. While looking round the delicatessen yesterday I spotted some mealy puddings, the first I had seen since my visit to Scotland. I bought one and boiled it for my breakfast this morning, but it had none of the magic of the Scottish mealy; it was too dry and had little flavour. A disappointment.

After lunch Richard and I drove out to visit Alastair in his rented farmhouse; a big house set among fields and meadows. We took a walk along muddy lanes lined with flowering betony, and into a dark, damp beech wood. The floor of the wood was thick with leaves and moss, a perfect site for fungi, and we found several species – especially great numbers of russula. The wood was quiet, eerie and cavernous, like a vast natural cathedral.

The weather began to get worse with drizzling rain and wind, and soon a cloudburst was upon us. Fortunately we were safe in the pub before the really heavy rain began, and decided to wait for a break before we drove to Berkhamsted.

Monday 19 August. Back to Suffolk with Richard. A beautiful, clear day, which improved as we moved towards East Anglia. For supper, Rose had secured the first runner beans of the year, and we ate these with a shepherd's pie.

Had to make a journey along the lanes after supper, and noticed some interesting roadside specimens: large parasol mushrooms, fully opened, and abundant wood sage in flower. The first blackberries beginning to ripen in the hedgerows. Many midges and thunder-flies in the air.

Thursday 22 August. Richard and I had planned on having a meal out, and we decided to try the Dutch Barn in Southwold. There are very few good restaurants in our area, but friends have consistently given very good recommendations about the Dutch Barn, so we went there full of anticipation, and were not disappointed.

We were not sure how formal the place was, so I wore a tie, and Richard was loaned a pony-club tie by Rose, which he rolled up and kept in his pocket in case it was needed. The restaurant itself was hidden away at the back of the town, overlooking the marshes. It was a large, high-ceilinged place, with simple tables spaced well apart; in the centre of the room a huge, heavy antique table held cheeses and fruit. A startling contrast. The atmosphere was friendly, informal, but somehow sedate and extremely comfortable; beautiful waitresses moved slowly and confidently around the restaurant, with long dresses and persuasive smiles. The pace was slow; we would not hurry this meal.

Before beginning we had a drink at the little bar in the corner of the restaurant, and perused the hand-written menu; we were glad to see that there was only a small list of dishes. Richard was overpowered by a dry martini cocktail, prepared with masterly skill by the cook's wife. We eventually moved to one of the tables and had our first course; I chose cold smoked mackerel while Richard had mushrooms *à la grecque*. The mushrooms themselves had obviously been marinaded in wine for they had a strange sparkling taste. After finishing this course we waited, but the gap between the courses was perfectly timed; we had long enough to savour and talk about the first course, and just as we began to long for more food it arrived. Here were all the best features of restaurant cooking, so often lacking these days: simple, imaginative dishes, subtlety, no flamboyant or useless garnishes or decoration, in all a meal that was unhurried and directed with good sense and understanding. It had all the virtues of the best home dinner parties. The most impressive part was the attention to small details, like the waitresses leaving vegetables in their dishes on the table rather than clumsily spooning the whole lot onto one's plate. In our case the vegetables were boiled new potatoes, runner beans and a dish of courgettes and onions finely chopped and cooked in butter. I had *noisette* of lamb cooked with herbs and Richard settled for pork *Provençale*. The lamb was a masterpiece; the gentle flavour of the herbs had penetrated right into the meat, and by a bit of culinary detective work I found that the cook had put a layer of ground black pepper and herbs between the meat and its protective fat. Superb skill and cunning. We were both astonished and overwhelmed by the excellence of the meal.

After this I only wanted a little Stilton and coffee, but Richard ordered some home-made almond ice-cream for himself. They provided coconut fudge with the coffee, and for a second I thought this might be a rare kind of sugar, but realized my error before actually putting a piece into my coffee.

We were the last in the place, and it was soon time to go. We thanked the cook and his wife, and then Richard drove recklessly along the sandy track past the quayside to the Harbour Inn, and then home.

Saturday 24 August. Tied my onions into bunches and hung them outside our door, under the porch.

Wednesday 28 August. There are signs of a sugar shortage – panic buying, hoarding, unofficial rationing by shopkeepers, rising prices. This is rather annoying to us, but only because it will disrupt our jam-making. Otherwise sugar is the classic non-essential food, and it is hard to understand what all the fuss is about.

Tuesday 3 September. The crops of autumn fruit this year are amazing. Elders dripping with clusters of dark berries; vast numbers of hips and haws and also lots of blackberries. But although these are covering the hedgerows the fruit seems to be smaller and harder than usual; perhaps there are more 'dewberries' this year.

Friday 6 September. Exceptionally good sausages from the local butcher; they were large and meaty and did not shrink or burst when they were cooked. Ate them with piles of fresh runner beans.

Wednesday 11 September. A bright and hazy autumn evening, many pheasants in the air. The smell of leaves and bonfires.

Tuesday 17 September. The recent good weather has meant that the autumn fruit and vegetables are thriving. I have been watching the raspberries in one of my gardens; there will be a good picking this weekend when Richard S. is visiting. There are also some ripe strawberries; this is the first time I have seen two crops in one year.

Marrows and runner beans are continuing to grow in profusion.

Thursday 19 September. Rose made some grapefruit marmalade for the weekend, using a quick and inexpensive method.

I felt cold for the first time today.

Saturday 21 September. Pouring rain all day. Had arranged to meet Richard S. in the Hart where I was working at lunchtime.

But by 2 o'clock he still hadn't arrived, and looking at the weather I expected him to be very late. But then he appeared, thirsty and hungry. He had taken a detour on his journey to pick some fresh figs from his father's garden, but he arrived too late for pub food, so he had to console himself with gin and crisps at the bar.

After closing time we drove to Southwold and we hurried around the town, both of us huddled under a single umbrella. I had to hunt for the olives and sea salt that I needed, but at last I found everything and we made our way back to the cottage. I noticed that Richard's car was loaded up with a mass of bulging white plastic carrier bags, and he was very secretive about the contents. He also hinted that he had some things maturing over the car engine; these turned out to be avocado pears, and when we got in I transferred these to our airing-cupboard, and tucked the fruit round the pipes of the immersion heater.

Before starting work on the meal we sat down and had tea and some fruit cake that Rose had made. At last Richard decided it was time to begin, and he heaved a leg of lamb out of one of the bags and proceeded to stab and gash it with a knife; he stuffed the holes with coriander seeds that he had crushed with our rolling pin.

He was admiring his efforts when we received a phone call. It was Rosemary saying that they were having problems finding a babysitter and might not be able to join us for the meal; I tried to keep Richard calm, but by this time he was convinced that the entire meal was doomed, and that more disasters would follow. But Rose arrived home and was full of ideas and suggestions, and we soon had the matter settled. Richard was still stalking about the kitchen nervously, chain-smoking and full of dismal prophesies about the food. He prepared a vast amount of waxy, yellow-podded french beans and put potatoes in the oven to roast. Then we waited.

Rosemary and John arrived, and Richard vanished into the kitchen; we pulled the dividing curtains so that he could do his work in secret. I refilled his glass through the curtains when it was empty. Before long everything was ready and we sat down to a salad of chopped avocado pear and smoked salmon moistened with lemon juice. This was a chunky salad – the avocados were perfect after their artificial ripening and the salmon was some of the pinkest and meatiest I have eaten. Richard was visibly pleased by the reaction to this course, and was soon in remarkable commanding form, really directing the meal. Then the lamb and vegetables appeared. The joint had a strong aromatic smell to it, and it carved perfectly. Thick tender slices with just the right scent and spicy flavour.

To finish the meal we had brown and white figs, fresh greengages and Camembert with strong coffee and some orange liqueur that Rosemary and John had donated. Richard seemed to drink this by the glassful, like wine. But he was relaxed, pleased and satisfied with his work; he slumped contentedly in the settee.

Sunday 22 September. Another sudden change in the weather. The morning bright, sunny and crisp with frost. Treated Richard to one of our famous Suffolk breakfasts: local kippers followed by toast with Rose's grapefruit marmalade.

It was my turn to cook today, so we went out to collect a few necessary items that I needed for lunch. Richard put on his Wellington boots and we went down to the Blyth estuary to see if there was any samphire worth picking; we found a big patch surrounded by slippery mud, and were soon pulling up the plants, our clothes and hands covered with seaweed and slime. We picked a bagful and then ambled back along the water's edge; it was a perfect morning, the water clear and glistening, birds everywhere – oystercatchers, redshanks, gulls. The meadows were green and wet with dew.

Then into the village to pick the raspberries and strawberries I had been saving; I also twisted a couple of large courgettes from their plants. Next stop the pub to have a drink and to cadge half a bottle of white wine for my cooking.

Back to the cottage to begin the lunch. I started the meal with a dish of samphire, then whiting cooked whole in white wine with herbs and olives and served with courgettes, runner beans and *sauté* potatoes. Finally a dessert of fresh raspberries and strawberries with cream. It went well although cooking conditions were cramped and Rose had to get Hannah's lunch while I was still at the stove. And Hannah pestered us after she had finished her meal and tipped a mountain of sugar onto Richard's fruit.

Richard left for London soon after lunch, and missed the real disaster of the weekend. Rose had been lent a horse box, the old type like a big cattle lorry. I was sitting indoors when suddenly I heard a dreadful sound; I looked out to see our already contorted wrought-iron archway being further flattened by the ramp and back end of the horse box which had somehow sheared off. Not funny. Fortunately there were no people or cars about and no horses inside the box. But it meant that about six of us had to spend the next two hours with ropes and hammers trying to dis-

mantle the back end of the box completely. But eventually the job was done, and although Rose was quite shaken, she calmed down later in the evening. It was a truly catastrophic finish to the weekend.

Monday 23 September. Weather bad again. It was too wet for me to go out gardening in the morning, so I decided to make soup instead. I had a couple of pounds of old, bulging french beans that were no good for eating fresh, so I chopped these up, fried them gently and then boiled them with some bacon pieces. It was a creamy yellow soup after I had thickened it, and I fried some bacon very crisp to eat with it.

It made a filling lunch for Rose, Hannah and myself, before I ventured out to do some work.

Thursday 26 September. For supper fried pig's liver with vegetables again.

Saturday 28 September. Rose had bought a lean piece of rolled brisket which we were hoping would last us two days. But then she invited a couple of friends to supper unexpectedly and we had to put the whole piece into one meal. I had plans for salting and spicing the meat, but these had to be abandoned, although I did rub it with crushed juniper berries and allspice before slowly baking it.

Luckily the food was good for there was no drink in the house. The meat was rather lean for brisket; I always think this cut is best when it is interlayered with fat. Very lean joints of brisket are often rather dry. I cooked the mixture of chopped courgettes and onions that I have become very fond of since that memorable meal at the Dutch Barn.

Thursday 3 October. The sound of guns in the evening. The pheasant-shooting season has begun.

Saturday 5 October. I had promised Gordon that I would cook him a Middle Eastern meal before he moved to Cambridge to take up his new musical appointment, and we agreed that it should be tonight. By working steadily through the afternoon I managed to prepare two *hors d'oeuvres* and a main course. The kitchen smelled of lemons and coriander.

The first dish, and really the most surprising, was an imitation *hummus*, using lentils instead of chick-peas. I blended the cooked lentils with a little olive oil, lemon juice and ground coriander, and liquidized the mixture very roughly; curiously the lentils changed colour and finally looked like a true *hummus*, creamy white. I served this dish alongside some raw mushrooms marinaded in oil and thyme, and at the last minute moistened, again with lemon juice.

By the time Gordon and Elizabeth arrived with a bottle of Bull's Blood, the lentils and mushrooms were cooling in the fridge, and a chicken was roasting in the oven; I had stuffed this with a mixture of dried fruit – apricots, prunes, raisins, etc. There was also rice, decorated and flavoured with fresh green herbs – fennel, thyme, lemon thyme, chives and mint, and a cauliflower cooked with lemon juice. This not only gave the cauliflower itself a pinkish appearance, but it provided a sharp tinge to the flavour; very unusual.

Rose hurried together a delicious chiffon using the remains of lemons left over from my dishes, and she succeeded despite the fact that Hannah stole some eggs from the table and dropped them onto the floor.

It was certainly one of the most successful meals that we have cooked; I could find no fault in it, and as a treat for Gordon it served its purpose well.

Wednesday 9 October. Given a large cock pheasant that had been killed on the road. It seemed to be quite undamaged and I hung it up from our oak beam to ripen.

Friday 11 October. Rose devised a simple and cheap supper: kippers with a sauce of chopped hard-boiled eggs. It was a delicious combination – the pale yellow sauce, very thick and heaped alongside the fish.

Saturday 12 October. The trees and hedgerows are almost bare. Boys are throwing sticks into the horse-chestnut at the end of our garden, to bring down the last conkers. The first sugar-beet lorries are here.

Very cold, with a vicious easterly wind; a time for fires and sweaters. Winter will soon be with us, and I suspect it may be a fierce one.

Tuesday 15 October. I spent the evening plucking and gutting the pheasant that has been hanging in our living-room. This time the smell was not too bad, and the job was easily done. We will cook the bird tomorrow.

Wednesday 16 October. Roasted the pheasant with bacon. It was a large fleshy bird, and when eating it we had no fear of cracking our teeth on lead shot embedded in the meat. The suspicion of shot always lessens my enjoyment of a pheasant. Ate it with crisp white cabbage, roast potatoes and rowan jelly.

Thursday 17 October. Rose boiled up the remains of the pheasant carcase to make stock, and she pulled the first of our beetroot. By the time I came back from gardening she had prepared a thick soup from the stock and the roots; it was bright crimson and quite substantial enough for a whole meal, but on this occasion it was only a prelude to a heavy steamed haggis.

Saturday 19 October. Many local farmers are fearful of the coming winter. A poor harvest has meant a shortage of natural fodder for the cattle, and the price of artificial feed is now enormous. They are beginning to talk of slaughtering beasts before they starve. We are almost returning to the medieval custom of autumn killing; of course there isn't an exact parallel, but the signs of imminent shortage and austerity are becoming more definite each day. We will soon have to learn how to live within limits; all of us may have to forget about extravagance and luxury, and think again about resourcefulness and economy.

I have also heard from fishermen that the herring season is very disappointing, and this is confirmed by the price and size of the fish in the shops; they hardly resemble the large and famous East Anglian autumn herring.

Wednesday 23 October. We had a very old tough boiling chicken which Rose put into a large pot to cook with lentils, root vegetables and some of my dried champignons. It was an extremely thick stew and very rich; the champignons softened well, turned a dark colour after long cooking, and the flavour was quite strong.

Friday 25 October. I have been doing quite a lot of gardening in Blythburgh recently, and I usually have lunch in the White Hart. Here they now offer such things as hot Cornish pasties and jacket potatoes. A couple of pints of bitter with a big potato moistened with butter is my usual lunch; it is substantial enough to keep me going through the afternoon.

At the moment the weather is very unpredictable, often changing from bright sunshine in the morning to rain after mid-day. But I have managed to do many of the necessary autumn gardening jobs – digging, clearing, staking plants against the wind.

Saturday 26 October. During the summer the jazz band began to get out of hand; too many musicians were coming and going, and there was antagonism inside the band itself. So John and I joined up with some of the more disgruntled members to form a new band. We had to begin practising simple numbers without a drummer or banjo player, but after several weeks we have started to improve, and tonight we gave our first public performance with a full band. The pub rocked with the music – we were surprised and excited to find how well we played. Drank a great deal and feasted on sausages and hard-boiled eggs before going home.

Monday 28 October. Another pheasant, this time a small hen bird, yet one more road casualty.

Sunday 3 November. Given a large piece of loin of lamb by Mac which should last us several days. Cut off two thick chops for our supper and ate them with fried potato scallops; the fat delicious.

Monday 4 November. A cold, damp day. The trees and hedgerows are bare and leafless except for clusters of dark red haws and a few orange rose hips.

Home from a dreary day's gardening to another supper of lamb chops – two more cut off the vast piece that we were given. There are occasions when there is no time to experiment or put variety into food, but these chops were so good simply fried that it was no injustice to repeat the meal.

Wednesday 6 November. Put the remainder of the loin of lamb to stew with root vegetables and lentils.

Saturday 9 November. Overheard in the White Hart at lunchtime: 'But you can't possibly have shepherd's pie; it's right at the bottom of the social scale!'

I came home in time for tea, and got to work on a bag of pink shrimps. I didn't bother to peel them clean, but only pulled off the heads and tails, and dug out any eggs. Then I crunched the meat and shell together.

Tuesday 12 November. Some time ago Rose stored a hock of fresh pork and a trotter in a friend's freezer. Today it was removed and left to thaw out for our supper.

Rose was occupied with Hannah, so I took charge of the meal. I boiled up the hock and trotter with onions and juniper berries, and then threw in some dried butter beans to thicken and flavour the mixture. The pot then simmered for a long time. Fortunately the butter beans softened well even though I hadn't soaked them. In fact we must have had the beans for more than two years, yet they seem to have improved in flavour and texture during that time.

When the supper was ready and the meat was falling from the bones, I divided it up and put the trotter aside for tomorrow. The meat itself was soft and tasted rather like boiled fowl, tinged with the aroma of juniper. The bean broth was so sticky and gelatinous that the remains had set in the saucepan even before we had finished eating.

Wednesday 13 November. Picked at the cold pig's trotter.

Thursday 14 November. A heavy frost early morning. The weather is getting colder. As I biked to work I could feel that characteristic tightening of the muscles which is the natural reaction to the cold and icy wind. By the end of my journey I had watering eyes and burning ears.

The weather has not been good recently, so I have been working indoors; I am now a painter. But I have kept an eye on the gardens, and I have noticed that the crab-apple trees are fully ripe; curiously the yellow crabs have almost all been taken by birds, while the red fruit still bend the branches of the neighbouring tree like heavy ripe cherries. I must pick some of these for pickling.

Had the first sprouts of the year for supper; they were small and firm but had been attacked by frost.

Saturday 16 November. In Berkhamsted for the weekend; a day of bright autumn sunshine. Berkhamsted is at its best at this time of year; the high street pavements covered with wet leaves, the chilly stroll to the pub, the ritual of the Saturday lunchtime pints. Then back home – always late – to one of Mum's inspired lunches. Today we had a beef stew with dumplings and whole onions. Richard had bought a jar of Dijon mustard which we had with the meal.

Richard and I went for an early evening Indian meal, and decided on a big selection of different dishes: *tandoori* chicken which was crisp and bright red on the outside with aromatic, almost creamy flesh inside, prawn *bhuna*, *sag bhaji*, *methi ghosht*, rice, pappadoms and *nan*. We ate this in leisurely fashion like a Chinese feast, picking from the various dishes.

Then afterwards, very full, we visited Richard G. who had invited us to drink *sake* with him; his house was reverberating with the music of Bruckner. He quickly produced the bottle and three small glasses. The *sake* was warm, but it needs to be so, for as soon as it cools it begins to taste like inferior surgical spirit. I jokingly said that I would prefer a pint of brown ale, so Richard, taking me at my word, went off and returned with an opened bottle. I refused it, but he poured it out and unflinchingly used it as a chaser for his *sake*. He has an extraordinary capacity for and resistance to mixed drinks.

After four glasses we decided we had drunk enough, and wandered across the churchyard to the pub.

Sunday 17 November. For lunch a young leg of lamb with roast potatoes, leeks and carrots. Mum had forgotten how many potatoes I usually eat and had only allowed three for my portion; not nearly enough.

In the evening my brother and I arranged to go up to the Five Bells for some Ruddles bitter. But outside it was pouring with rain; this was unexpected because we could not detect any signs of wind or rain from inside the house. Drove along already flooded roads; a torrent of water coming down the rough track that leads to the pub. Feared that we might be stranded. But we made it and the Ruddles was at its best, not too syrupy.

Monday 18 November. To London with Richard. A dismal, dark day. Spent about an hour at lunchtime, wandering around Soho, trying to decide where to eat; Richard had little money, and I had even less. Eventually agreed on a cheap kebab. The place had no licence, which was a pity, since it is almost essential to drink red wine with kebabs. The food was good, although I'm not in favour of the habit of removing the meat from the skewers before serving. Much of the pleasure of kebabs lies in the act of sliding each piece of meat off the skewer, sniffing the smoky aroma and then tasting it. Without the skewer, the kebab is little more than a jumbled collection of bits. Rather bland olives with the meal.

Back to Berkhamsted for a supper of cold lamb, jacket potatoes and an unusual salad of tomatoes and raw leeks sliced.

Tuesday 19 November. Drove to Suffolk with Richard. Weather much better, cold but bright and clear. Bought some smoked mackerel in Southwold, and spent the evening drinking 'Old' in the White Hart; the Old is Adnams strong winter mild and is probably like the original beer of the area.

We tried the mackerel when we got back, slicing pieces off it like smoked salmon.

Wednesday 20 November. Had the mackerel grilled for breakfast – very meaty. Hannah thought they were superb, and I ended up forgoing half my fish, even though she had already eaten her breakfast.

The weather turned again; a day of torrential rain, gales and flooding. By the middle of the afternoon the roads were awash, the drains were overflowing and the rain seemed to be worsening. Rose went out in the car in the evening and got stuck; the lane between Wenhaston and Bramfield was completely under water and she had to be towed to safety. But on her return journey she took the same route, and was stranded again. She arrived home well after midnight, completely soaked.

Friday 22 November. Rose to Cambridge for the weekend to visit Gordon and Elizabeth. After painting all day, I biked home, taken with an obsessive desire to have a convenience packet meal for my supper. This was partly laziness, but also I wanted to try these foods, to see what they were really like. I had tasted them before and they had been disastrous; but for some reason I felt that they might have improved over the years. I can't explain this.

I bought myself a packet of 'chop suey'. The packaging and ingredients should have been enough to scare me off: a packet of rice, a packet of dried meat and vegetables, a sachet of sweet-and-sour sauce and finally some transparent noodles. The contents were extraordinary, no mention of anything like bamboo shoots or bean sprouts, but plenty of swedes, peas and beans. Even before beginning to cook, I was annoyed; my small obsession seemed bound to lead to a bad meal. Still I went ahead, as the packet instructed, and prepared the meat and vegetables. This resulted in little more than a packet soup – minestrone was the nearest analogy I could think of – with strange porous cubes of meat-like substance in it. These cubes had no fibre, no meaty texture, and they tasted like flavoured blotting-paper. Then as the rice cooked, I squirted the sachet of sauce into the 'soup', and fried up the noodles; these were most unpleasant, bright yellow and fatty.

Having gone through all the different stages of preparation, I was determined to at least try the result. It was far worse than I could have imagined; I ended up eating the rice and tipping most of the noodles and sauce straight into the dustbin.

I felt unwell after the meal, and had to take a couple of indigestion tablets before going out to play jazz.

Saturday 23 November. After serving in the White Hart at lunch-time, I went to Southwold to get some food for the weekend; bought a piece of smoked haddock, very pale and soft to the touch, and a cherry yoghurt for my breakfast tomorrow.

Back to the Hart for an early evening drink and something to eat. The pub dominated by tired aristocrats from a shooting party. They were noisy and at first made me uneasy with their loud chatter. But they were courteous and civilized, and mellowed much with drinking; a rare change from some of the customers I see in the pub. After several Broadsides, I chose a neat snack of *rollmop* herrings with a couple of segments of tomato and French bread; I scrounged some extra lemon for the fish from the bar.

Then biked to Rosemary's for the evening, my head numb.

Sunday 24 November. Up very late for me – 10 o'clock. Ate the yoghurt and steamed the smoked haddock in milk and butter with a little black pepper. The fish was very good, mildly smoked and very sweet. But nothing can quite equal the taste of that rich fish liquor, which as a boy I would drink off heavy fish knives. It never tasted quite right from a spoon – like drinking wine out of paper cups. There was some quality in the shape, surface and weight of the knife that made it ideal for the task, but today I had to be content with a spoon.

Wednesday 27 November. It is surprising how many people distrust or dislike coley. Rose and I eat it quite often and for fish pies and the like it has much more flavour than cod. But it is not pure white, it's a bloody fish with grey-pink flesh, which presumably makes people suspicious; they associate whiteness with freshness in all fish. Coley also has the reputation of being 'catfish'; in fact we have actually been asked by a fishmonger whether we were buying it for ourselves or for a cat.

Tonight we had a pie made from the fish. It was flaked in a cheese sauce with sliced hard-boiled eggs, and covered with creamed potatoes. The murky colour of the fish disappears when it is cooked, and it looks as white as any cod or haddock.

Monday 2 December. The ground is very wet. I went into the garden to pull some of our leeks; they came up easily, but they had a coating of sticky mud.

Thursday 5 December. During the day I had a premonition of oxtail, and phoned Richard to suggest it as a lunch this Saturday, when I shall once again be in Berkhamsted. But he was out, and the message was not delivered.

Friday 6 December. This week the bakers have been on strike, and there has been no flimsy factory bread, although small bakers are still working, making what is called 'specialist' bread. This has given rise to a remarkable return to home-baking; our local shop which normally sells about three packets of yeast in a week apparently sold its entire stock of forty-eight packets in one day.

Saturday 7 December. Last night I played in the jazz band and did not get home until well after midnight with a headache from poor-quality keg beer.

Left for Berkhamsted at 5.30 in the morning, after a breakfast of bacon, eggs and coffee. Biked in the moonlight to Darsham station to get the first train to Ipswich. It was very clear, almost like day, and with a cool breeze that cleared my head, so that I was wide awake by the time the train arrived. I watched the dawn break as I sat in the station café at Ipswich, drinking a weak, sickly cup of coffee. Then the train to Chelmsford and finally the tedious journey across country to Tring on the coach. Noticed cables of red and orange bryony berries tangled among hawthorn bushes.

Finally reached Tring and caught a double-decker bus to Berkhamsted. I had forgotten how excellent these vehicles were, with their rattling tartan-covered seats and primitive bell cord. This part of the journey transformed me; I felt bright and lively and was glad to be back in the town. I met Richard and Alastair in the Swan and discovered to my real astonishment that there *was* oxtail for lunch. This was surely a good omen. The oxtail was exactly as I remembered it, big pieces, the meat barely clinging to the bones after its long cooking and with that characteristic stickiness. A bowl in the middle of the table held the bones after they had been sucked clean. I seasoned the stew with Worcester sauce, which helped to clear my head; the beer in the Swan was not at its best, and this plus the delayed effect of the journey was making my head throb.

During the afternoon I felt progressively worse, and was doubtful if I would be able to cope with the evening – Richard and I were due to go to Justin's with Mouse and Alan for supper. So I dosed myself with tablets, and was definitely cheered by seeing Alan again; eventually, by the time we got to Justin's, I was feeling bland, but not actually ill. Two large whisky-and-sodas revived me and I was able to enjoy the evening.

We began our meal with Jerusalem artichoke soup, smooth and light brown, and eaten with a lump of home-made soda bread sliced and spread with warm garlic butter. Then beef casseroled with wine and herbs; with this we drank some very good *vin ordinaire* out of heavy glass goblets. In fact the whole meal was dominated by utensils – the goblets, large ornate knives and forks, big earthenware dishes.

It was an excellent evening, and it was good to see Justin again; his sanity is reassuring in these times.

Sunday 8 December. The artichokes affected me even more than parsnips; unbelievable wind. Before I got up in the morning I heard Richard at work downstairs, beating a Yorkshire pudding with his usual skill.

For lunch, roast topside of beef with Yorkshire pudding, roast potatoes and leeks. As always the Yorkshire was cooked under the meat so that it soaked up the juices that dripped from it, and when ready it was cut up into pieces. Always in my childhood there were battles and arguments as to who would get which piece; those from the centre of the pudding were moist and soaked in bloody juice, while the outside pieces were dry and had a crisp brown crust where they met the tin. I could never really decide which I preferred, although on balance I think I favoured the moist pieces marginally. Today I sampled both sorts.

In the evening I mentioned plans that I had been forming for a supper on Boxing Day. I want to prepare a piece of spiced beef, with a rough pâté, some pickles – probably crab-apples and Jerusalem artichokes – and a kedgeree; also I want Richard to make an elaborate salmagundi or salad. A real English cold stand.

Monday 9 December. Back in Suffolk. The weather bitterly cold.

Wednesday 11 December. An icy morning. Biked to work through the first flakes of snow, but before long the wind increased to a gale, and I was battling against a blizzard. I was unable to continue so I ran for shelter behind a tree until there was a lull. A sheer blanket of snow was blowing viciously across the open fields; birds swooped, unable to cope with the wind, and cattle in the meadows looked suddenly lean and hungry.

After lunch the snow turned to sleet, and then it stopped.

Thursday 12 December. For breakfast a large bowl of porridge covered with golden syrup. Then to Norwich for the day, to work

in the library and to hunt for some mustards that I want to give Richard as a present for Christmas. The Mustard Shop was closed so I had to wander round the city in the rain, and called at several shops before I found what I wanted.

Lunch in a Chinese restaurant. For just over 50p a reasonable meal – chicken and sweet-corn soup followed by *char siu chow mein*. But I avoided the English sweet which I knew from past experience was likely to ruin any enjoyment or satisfaction that I had gained from the rest of the meal.

Friday 13 December. Picked a bag full of red crab-apples to take to Berkhamsted for pickling.

Saturday 14 December. Played in the band at Haddiscoe. It was a private party for a cricket club, in a place like a miniature holiday camp with chalets and caravans; the guests in party hats were baffled by the sound of an eight-piece jazz band, but we gradually won them over as they drank and began to dance.

We had been promised a turkey dinner, but ended up being escorted into the kitchen during the interval for soggy cheese sandwiches and coffee. In fact the meal had been roast beef, and the remnants were scattered around the kitchen: the joint, some cold roast potatoes and french beans that were turning yellow as they steeped in a saucepan of tepid water.

Although we had originally expected to play for about one hour, we continued till after midnight – two and a half hour's playing in all. Exhausted by the end.

Sunday 15 December. Down to Berkhamsted to begin my Christmas break. I was hungry when I got in, so Mum heated up a plate of

Sunday lunch for me: roast lamb, potatoes, carrots. I ate this with a tray on my lap while listening to Tony Hancock on the radio. Finished with a fat slice of bread pudding – a solid fawn-coloured mass with juicy raisins and sultanas, and smelling of cloves and nutmeg.

I felt lively and exuberant in the evening, but Richard was badly depressed and drinking a great deal of whisky.

Thursday 19 December. Richard improving. Have managed to interest him in my plans for an English supper.

Bought a very large smoked mackerel (it weighed nearly a pound without the head) in an attempt to cheer Richard up. It had been hot smoked, so the flesh was cooked, and we had half a fish each for our supper. It succeeded in reviving Richard.

Friday 20 December. In the afternoon I went into the town to buy the ingredients for my pickles and also to select a suitable piece of beef for spicing. I found a good bit of topside, nearly 3 lbs, lean and well shaped for salting.

Then back for a supper of mince on a bed of fried rice and peas before beginning my tasks. First the beef. I began the process by rubbing it all over with brown sugar; it was good to get to grips with the meat after so long thinking about it. I put it into a pot, covered it and stored it in the meat safe. Then I started on the pickled crab-apples. I chose the best and cooked them very gently so that the skins did not crack. They lost colour quickly, which was a pity, but after straining and pickling them in wine vinegar with sugar and spices, they looked pink and attractive.

My last job was to pickle the Jerusalem artichokes. These were not too difficult to peel, but I fear that I may have slightly overcooked them. They were pickled in wine vinegar with strips of lemon peel.

After a last look at the beef I went out to the pub to have a drink with Alastair.

Saturday 21 December. In the morning I went out to do some shopping. A windy, blustery day and the town very full. I enjoy open-air shopping – the rough displays, the smells, searching for bargains and shouting my orders. But the same crowds and activity in the supermarket I find intolerable.

Back home my main job after lunch was to salt the beef. I ground up the sea salt, spices (have been unable to find any juniper berries as yet), and saltpetre, and rubbed this mixture into the meat; the sugar had already given it a brown sticky appearance. From now on I shall have to attend to the meat each day, rubbing and turning it.

Later I wandered into the town again, this time with Richard; he called at the wine shop to order the Christmas bottles – some decent sherry, claret, port, etc.

Tuesday 24 December. The final shopping expedition. Richard and I went out in the morning to collect all the supplies we still needed for the holiday. And we called at the butcher's shop to pick up the Christmas Day capon and a piece of boiling bacon; an essential and enjoyable task. We also searched the delicatessen for a few choice items: some Bel Paese cheese, bilberries in syrup, rare chutneys, etc.

Then to the Swan for lunchtime drinks, a couple of gins on the house and then the usual pints. Christmas Eve always brings the anticipation of old friends, chance encounters, dramas. Quite heavy drinking, everyone in the pub except Alan.

Back home at closing time to unload the supplies and rub the beef. It felt soft and spongy and was bathed in a thick liquor of blood, sugar and salt. It will be quite exceptional I think. A pungent, aromatic smell. Carols on the radio.

The old ritual of the Christmas Eve drinking session seems to have lost its appeal. The pub unpleasantly crowded – sharing seats, rowdiness and we searched in vain for some friend to appear. Only late in the evening did Mouse's sister, Jo, turn up briefly. By this time we were past caring, Alan drinking from his immense pewter quart mug, his brilliant humour disintegrating into boyish vulgarity. But the jokes kept us joyful and inebriate, although the evening was something of an anti-climax. Perhaps I have simply forgotten what these sessions used to be like.

Wednesday 25 December. A dreary morning, but extraordinarily mild. Cloudy, with rain in the air. Up late after present-opening to a breakfast of cold ham and hard-boiled eggs. Mum was busy in the kitchen, and declined any assistance from the family, so we lounged in the sitting-room, eating nuts and drinking sherry. Traditionally our Christmas lunch is eaten very late, and today we did not begin before 3.30.

Richard carved the capon, and we ate sausages, roast potatoes, sprouts, peas and stuffing with it. The capon itself was moist and sweet, better even than chicken or turkey. The bottle of wine – Pouilly Fumé – which Richard had secured from the wine shop was a perfect light wine for the meal. We finished with slices from a dark Christmas pudding, and then slumped into armchairs.

In the evening we nibbled at mince pies and later had plates of cold capon, ham and pickles. But Richard and I were thirsty, and, with no beer in the house, we had to be content with the remains of the wine left over from lunch. But it did little to quench our thirsts and we went to bed still with dry mouths. A restful, if rather undistinguished day.

Thursday 26 December. A better morning, still very warm. Richard went out for a walk and came back with over thirty species of wild flowers and a twig of hawthorn almost in leaf. All signs of a severe winter have disappeared, and the mild weather is producing unnatural growth in plants and trees; bulbs are sprouting everywhere.

Another good lunch – cold capon and ham with salad and jacket potatoes, followed by solid cold Christmas pudding eaten with bilberries. Felt unwell during the afternoon, and I felt no better even after a glass of Grand Marnier liqueur (a present from Richard with echoes of a past Christmas when I received the same gift). I was worse in the evening; I fear the 'flu is upon me.

Friday 27 December. In bed all day; I definitely have the 'flu. Had to postpone the English supper planned for tomorrow; fortunately the spiced beef will keep in its marinade for quite some time.

Monday 30 December. Feeling much better. Cooked the beef. I cleaned the meat and wrapped it in foil before putting it into a pot with a little water, and I put another sheet of foil between the pot and its lid. During the cooking I checked the oven, but could detect no aromatic smells, so I knew the foil had completely sealed the meat.

When it was cooked I let it get cold and then pressed it, using an old iron for a weight.

Tuesday 31 December. At last the day of the supper. Seeing the quality of the spiced beef, I was confident that it would be a memorable evening.

In the morning Richard and I went out to buy the ingredients we still needed, then after a drink we rushed home to begin work. The beef was wrapped in its foil and only needed to be sliced, so I started on the devilled mixed meats (2 lbs of chicken, salt pork and bacon pieces for 60p) and a kedgeree. Richard meanwhile was doing amazing things with more than twenty ingredients for his salmagundi. It was a huge bed of chopped lettuce and chicory in which were hidden almonds, olives and pieces of orange, and set in this bed were scooped-out orange and grapefruit skins which acted as bowls for a series of miniature salads and fillings; the most unexpected was a combination of pulped gooseberries and anchovies. This was at the centre of the salmagundi.

As we worked through the afternoon the depression and lethargy of the 'flu disappeared; even the memories of an indifferent Christmas no longer bothered us. We were meeting the demands of the occasion with skill, imagination and enthusiasm. We were supremely confident.

Then I carved the beef and tried it. It looked like the best-quality ham with a warm, spicy aroma; it had somehow lost all connections with the original piece of beef, and was quite unlike anything I had tasted before, although as I cut towards the centre the softness and fibrous texture of beef returned. I offered it to our friends proudly.

The evening itself was dominated by the food and also by Alan's antics; he drank a great deal of wine and was cavorting wildly and blowing on a duck-caller. Everyone else was mellow, half way to drunkenness; Richard and I were particularly pleased that it had turned out well.

Looking at it, the occasion seemed to bring together all the feelings I have towards food: nostalgia for the food and eating habits of a generation with grander tastes than our own, the memories of my own past, the skills accumulated through the year and finally brought out and used to create a gathering, a feast for friends. Richard and I had used our skills well, we had solved problems, prevented disasters and had successfully transformed a potentially dour evening, ruined by illness and depression, into a memorable celebration. We could ask for no more.